A GI MACHINE GUNNER
From the Seminary to Korea's Front Line
1951 – 1952

This memoir is a recollection of events drawn from personal knowledge and experiences of the author while in the 1st gun squad, 3rd section of heavy 30 machine guns, Dog Company, 1st Battalion, 35th Regimental Combat Team, 25th Infantry Division in Korea from August 1951 through May, 1952. Human frailty has reaped its toll on this old soldier the years since combat, and I ask forgiveness if your recollections differ, none-the-less, weakness of memory a given, I write about those tough days. And I dedicate the memoir to all who served with me, in Dog and Charley Companies, and the 1st, 2nd and 3rd Battalions of the 35th RCT, 25th Infantry Division.

Especially in memory of those Killed in Action while serving with me: PFC Leonard J. Griscones, Dog Company; Private Alvin Jean Christy, Charley Company Corporal Michael C. Petruska, Charley Company

Copyright: James F. Walsh 2002

TRAVERSE AND SEARCH
A MEMOIR
By
JAMES F. WALSH

A GI MACHINE GUNNER
From the Seminary to Korea's Front Line
1951 – 1952

Contents

ENLISTMENT 7
DIGGING A LATRINE 14
SHIPBOARD BOXING 19
BATTLE FOR THE OUTPOST 22
SOLE SURVIVING SON 78
CREW DRILL 89
INCOMING 92
I REMEMBER OPERATION CACTI 95
OPERATION CACTI OFFICIAL REPORTS 109
OPERATION MESABI 112
WALKING THE DOG 118
COOTIE HUNT 119
RATS 122
TRUCE TALKS 124
A CHRISTMAS SONG 127
POW 128
MASH 137
NIGHT GUARD IN DOG TWO BUNKER 146
HOMECOMING 153
SEPARATION 155
ACKNOWLEDGEMENTS 156

ENLISTMENT

It wasn't easy joining the U. S. Army, or getting to the battlefront in Korea.

On its face all that was required of an American citizen to enlist in the Army was being of age, physically and mentally well, and signing the necessary papers. Then after successfully completing basic and advanced infantry training, receiving an order to ship out to Korea's MLR, (main line of resistance). Simple as that.

Not for me, Jim Walsh, who, when the war began, was a sprouting ecclesiastic.

After June 25, 1950, the U. S. Army's intended police action in the aid of South Korea's Army had erupted into a full scale war with the North Korean Peoples' Army. Our troops were being pushed back to the sea. Could they remain on the Korean peninsula? More soldiers were needed.

I was working that Summer as a counselor in a camp for boys, Camp Ozanam in Michigan, and that Fall, returning to college as a third year seminarian. I was deferred from the draft. Yet, teen-age hero worship of the men and women who'd lived in my Detroit neighborhood from 1943 to 1945 and had gone off to fight World War II in Europe and the Far East, motivated me. More so did older brother Jack. When of age he went into the Army and was shipped to Japan, albeit as a soldier of occupation.

Nineteen years of age, I wished to emulate Jack and neighborhood service men and women to do my patriotic duty for God, country and family, with a philosophical bonus, fighting the spread of atheistic communism.

Mom, Theresa Walsh, didn't agree with either emulated or philosophical motivations. She wanted my continuation of studies for the priesthood, ultimately becoming a pastor of souls in a Roman Catholic Parish. She argued a vast number of other young men had suddenly heard the Lord's trumpet since the outbreak of the War and eagerly answered the call to religious life.

Dad, Denis P. Walsh, didn't agree either. He utilized his most persuasive powers and otherwise did all possible to complicate the effort. The weight of his tongue about leaving the seminary wasn't easily sidestepped. He declared I was wrongly setting aside obedience to the Archbishop on behalf of President Harry Truman's political prattle, that my urge to enlist was theological mutiny! Why quit benefit of clergy?

My parents were quick with the turn of a phrase and never hesitated giving me a piece of mind. Mom, hair red as western clouds swimming in a setting sun, face freckled, was baptized Bridget, herself with the surname Walsh from south Ireland's Cashel Townland near Tobercurry in County Sligo. A downstairs maid for a wealthy Chicago family, her personal name was changed to Theresa, that she not seem so Irish.

Dad, hair black as peat, face limestone, came from a hard place, Loughguile, County Antrim in the North of Ireland where belief in God, whether preached by priest or minister, was sword enforced. When Nationalist of the South of Ireland agreed to partition southern counties from the six counties of the North, rather than suffer more grievously under the dominance of English Loyalists, Dad shipped out to Manitoba, Canada. He worked as a carpenter with his Uncle Charlie Connolly. Going to Chicago with an Irish football (soccer) team, he met the love of his life. He returned to Chicago twice more, the third time marrying Theresa in 1927. They became American citizens.

The tough financial years of the Depression caused Dad to go wherever construction was ongoing. His grasp of Mathematics, Physics, and Mechanical Engineering was on a par with Collegiate teaching faculty. It had to be to estimate and sell jobs to buyers. Then he'd do the work.

We moved from Chicago, Illinois in 1938 to Oklahoma City, Oklahoma.

In 1939, we moved to Dallas, Texas. If my red hair wasn't the flag, my Yankee accent was when taking a shortcut across the public school playground to get to St. Cecilia grade school.

Tough public schoolboys were alert to defend the doctrine of separation of Church and State. I was challenged to fight or circle the playground. I fought. Going home after another fistfight, I expected a strapping.

Dad's version of child rearing was simulating his were growing up in the north of Ireland focused on the 'Troubles'. Still, he guided us with a nimble spirit, with song, but that failing, with a horse-hide strap across the backside, the last swat more forceful than the first. When he said I hurled the fists of an embryo blacksmith with the instinct of an Irish wolfhound, it wasn't because I fought every public *school boy who'd challenged, but as if I'd laid it on the nose of himself, the Lord Protector, Oliver Cromwell. Throughout the year of the third grade, I had more fist fights than baseball games.*

Mom preferred I read books and turn my attention to matters intellectual and spiritual, not fist fights. She intervened. Her Friday afternoon home made donuts, public and parochial students alike to partake, brought a time out to frequent contentions.

We moved to Detroit, Michigan in 1943. There followed years of War News, radio's 'Jack Armstrong, All American Boy', football, basketball, baseball, hanging around with other paperboys, sipping pineapple sodas at the Biltmore Drugstore, reading comic books, talking of major league baseball players.

In 1948, Mom had wondered if Holy Mother Church's mission of sanctifying the ruthless was being advanced by a former prize fighter training the fists of the son who'd chosen the seminary. To her nothing was more eloquent than a modest seminarian, or more sublime than the study of Christ's teachings. Boxing appeared not too liturgical.

Dad had maintained my left jab, right cross, left hook and ring savvy extolled the brawn of St. Scholastica's grade school graduates, the intelligence of the Detroit Archdiocese's seminarians. He felt Gaelic-Celtic souls in Purgatory, few as there were, would find momentary relief in their longing for the sweet sounds of celestial harps by watching a descendant of Ireland's 12th Century invaders from Wales win the Novice light heavy weight championship of the Catholic Youth Organization. They did.

Under Benefit of Clergy but with guilt stained patriotism, I returned to the seminary. While my mind concentrated on studies, my emotions rode the tide at Inchon, South Korea, when on September 15, 1950, the U. S. Marines and the 7th Infantry Division hit the beaches. The North Korean Peoples' Army was caught off guard and driven back to and out of Seoul. Meanwhile, the U. S. Eighth Army broke out of the Pusan Perimeter, driving North toward the Yalu. All that seemed left to the War was a mopping up action. My turn to have served in the military had passed. So it seemed on November 24, 1950. Though there had been several sharp skirmishes with North Korean forces that included Chinese Volunteers, when the U. S. Eighth Army moved out on attack that day beyond North Korea's Capitol at P'yongyang it encountered only a few small enemy squad and platoon-sized groups employing small arms fire. It was soon thereafter, however, when hordes of Chinese Communist troops tore into the Eighth Army and X Corps north of the Chosin Reservoir. The U. S. Marines and 7th Division troops were encircled. They fought south, not north, to escape. The U. S. Eighth Army was driven back 275 miles south, the longest retreat in the annals of the U. S. Military.

I left the seminary and returned home.

Mom was succinct: "It's shameful throwing off black clerical garb for olive drab."

Dad's face redden before oxygen exploded from his lips. "You're daft, son, doubly so giving up both seminary and college deferments to fight in Harry

Truman's Asian War. Living in a seminary was a life in a flower bowl, in the army it's life in a piranha infested river. You'll be eaten alive! Why leave the study of cosmology, epistemology, Latin verbs and Logic for theories of weapon placement, covering fire and attack? Why go from philosophical library to a bunker, from prayers in the seminary's chapel to shell pocked ridges:

"It's my duty," I said, "to my Country. For God, I'll fight the spread of atheistic communism."

Dad looked the Archangel Michael about to slay the devil with a sword. "If it's a crusade you're after having for Country and God, you'll find it in County Antrim in the north of Ireland in the Irish Republican Army against Plantation Loyalists from England, a crusade any Irishman named Walsh could sink his teeth."

Instead, on February 6, 1951, I joined and within a few days I'd bit into U. S. Army chow. It wasn't as miserable as the sixteen weeks of infantry training under an irascible Commanding Officer, the C. O. of Company 'R', 516 Infantry Regiment at Camp Breckenridge, Kentucky. I survived him and his cadre and was ordered before a Board to determine candidates for Leadership School. All on the Board, except my CO who wrote my attitude was 'sloppy', saw me as a candidate. So the order was cut.

I didn't want to attend. I'd joined the Army to fight as an infantryman in Korea. More training turned me cold. I'd been in one school or another since age six, and needed no more theoretical concepts propounded by Officers like my CO. I wanted to go where men were men, or became men during a firefight. I appealed the order. Disgusted with me as much as with the Board who saw me as a leader, my CO had two Military Policemen march me to C&A, Classification and Assignment. I was, forthwith, ordered to Korea.

DIGGING A LATRINE

In early August 1951, the troop ship Marine Lynx ferried me and hundreds of other soldiers from Seattle, Washington across the Pacific Ocean to Japan. A train's passenger car, narrow as a toothpick, packed dozens of us replacements back to back as if four by four sticks of lumber, then raced across the land of the rising sun before the sun rose. Not a moment too long at an Army Supply Depot, I and a few others were hustled into a DC-3. It took off well enough but too soon landed at Kimpo air base in South Korea. That very afternoon, assigned to a frontline combat unit, Dog Company of the 35th Regimental Combat Team ("RCT"), 25th Infantry Division in the Eight US Army, United Nations Forces, I was hurriedly transported by an Army 2x2 truck to Kumhwa, North Korea. Amazed the Generals were in such haste to get me into combat on the front lines, and stupefied at the height of the mountains on which the war last month had been raged, it came as an immense relief to find the 35th RCT was in 25th Division reserve and not on the frontline.

Sleeping in a pup tent along side the pup tents of the troops of Dog Company's 3rd section of heavy machine guns, 1st Battalion, was definitely preferable to ducking incoming enemy shells within a foxhole's depth atop some bald hilltop a mile or so to the north. Rumors, as numerous as fleas in an Army blanket, told us the war was over given that the truce tent talks were ongoing between our side and the enemy's side, the North Korean, 'Imun Gun', and Chinese Communist Forces, 'CCF'. Even though I'd joined the Army in

February to fight Godless Communists, a truce was alright with me in August 1951 now that I was actually in a combat zone where there was fighting against such Godless Commies. It was easy to say back stateside "I looked forward to combat." While there were no drinking buddies or pretty girls to impress in North Korea, why be hard-headed about wanting to get into combat?

If our Divisional, Regimental, Battalion and Company Commanders believed the shooting war was coming to an end, it was evident they didn't want us over doing our sack time. Every morning we were sent out to climb one hill or another, there being no limit of high hills, up on which we trained: fire missions, squad tactics, gun drills and other soldiery things, (like climb-climb-climb for the sake of climbing) to keep in shape. Of the ten soldiers in the 1st machine-gun squad, 3rd Section, the squad leader, gunner, assistant gunner and seven ammo-bearers, I was the last ammo bearer. Each ammo bearer carried two cans of ammunition into action plus back pack, equipment and carbine. Challenged by the section's ammo bearers to run an uphill race with as much ammo in hand as possible, I lugged six cans, each weighing 20 pounds and holding 250 rounds, up a never ending climb to win the honor of 'first idiot ammo bearer', and from each of the other idiot ammo bearers, a beer (3.2% yet). It never crossed my mind there would be a later consequence.

Near Kumhwa, North Korea, in reserve behind the Main Line of Resistance, MLR, if there were a rooster around it would have been asleep when my squad leader, Staff Sergeant Dean Warren rustled me, his newest replacement, out of the sack. Privates Earl Diemer and Im Ta Song, (Joe ROK), a KATUSA, (Korean soldier assigned to the U. S. Army) were also summarily rustled to their feet. Warren gave signs for quiet. I dressed quickly wondering, with my heart pumping nervously, about the nature of this secretive mission. We followed the sergeant out of the tent. Where was he leading us on this pitch dark morning? KP?

Warren handed us shovels. "Follow the latrine manual, Walsh," he said, handing me the booklet. "You're in charge, so put the soakage pit at least a hundred yards from the mess tent. Hurry it up if you want chow. We got training to do. Gun drills on hill 523."

"Thanks a lot, Sarge," I answered with a hint of sarcasm. Another dirty detail to the heavy thirty machine gun squad's last three ammo bearers. We shouldered shovels. I was in command. My first! Joe ROK didn't read English and I doubted if Diemer could. The reason for my leadership rested on the fact that, with two years in seminary college, I might have been able to comprehend a manual on building urinals. That was the way it was in the Army. They had recognized my leadership skills and put them to use: leading the digging of a urinal pit.

"Come on," I said, as issuing an order just didn't occur to me. I led my crew through morning's first light a hundred yards north. "We'll dig a square pit," I said after consulting the manual, "4 feet by 4 feet." I stepped it off, four shoe lengths as the measure and marked the corners. "We dig 4 feet deep." I shoved my shovel into one corner. Joe ROK and Diemer dug at others. Dirt was turning when I saw an evil pointed face, a repulsive fat rat with a long nude tail. I'd ripped open a nest. A horde of rats flowed up like lava from a volcano squealing louder than Joe ROK. They attacked. I swung my shovel to ward one off. I slammed it on other rats. "Hit them Diemer! Joe! Just don't stand there."

Joe wacked away holding his ground but Diemer recoiled when a rat the size of a St. Bernard puppy leapt for his face. He bolted, the enormous rat in hot pursuit. I lit out after them to kill the rat. The speed of Diemer's sprint would have shamed a bullet. The rat was nearly as fast. I was breathing their dust. I had no idea a rat would chase a human being.

"Diemer," I yelled, "stay away from the tents."

He didn't. He bugged through the mess supply tent overturning cartons of fresh eggs. He headed for our tent. Unfortunately he charged into the wrong one and with him the rat. I was far behind. It couldn't have been a second before the inmates of that insane asylum, judging from the curses and crashing noises within, took notice of the rodent; not to mention the gasping Diemer, who not as quickly as he went in, backed out.

Facing him was a GI bigger than a jeep who bellowed, "I'm going stick you too, shovel-head." On the point of the jeep's bumper, a bayonet, was the squirming rat.

I arrived in time to pull Diemer from the meat on a stick; then improvised to calm the seething soldier. "Rat's big enough to eat GI rations without opening tin cans in the mess tent! Diemer ran it out." When something was overheard about deguting us foulups, I whispered, "walk away calmly, Diemer."As if he had the bowel-runs, he sprinted away. I, nonetheless, walked calmly, maintaining some dignity. I marveled over that rat's attraction toward the ammo bearer, something a hot shower might cure if Diemer ever was so inclined. He and his fatigues were always in need of a champion-hog scrubbing.

"Joe ROK," I said resuming command, "stay away from rat nests." Rather than rededicate my military career to chewing outs by my squad leader, I figured we better dig a pit somewhere. I found a place with no hint of rodent. We put down the four footer, filled it with loose stone around ventilating shafts and plugged in five pipe urinals seventy-five yards from the mess tent.

Why not? Who wanted a long walk to discharge army coffee?

SHIPBOARD BOXING

His trigger finger pointed like a bayonet. "You're Red from the boxing ring," the rifleman stated with finality, his M1 rifle slung from his left shoulder.

We, first machine gun squad, were setting up a squad tent.

"What you mean, boxing ring?" squad leader Staff Sergeant Dean Warren asked from the tent, looking from me to the rifleman.

He said, "I mean, I remember Red from boxing ring on the troop-ship, the Marine Lynx. I've been telling the squad about that big fight, and dog gone if here isn't Red. I'm Jean Christie from Charley Company, just over in that stand of trees a hundred yards to the north. Right next door to Dog Company." He aimed the trigger finger in that direction.

"Red Walsh," I said, shaking his hand.

"You hit that big guy with a mule's kick? Don't they know?"

They didn't, but I felt pleased as a monkey finding a banana Christie would tell them.

"Back on the troop ship," he said without hesitation, "there was a ring down in the hold. A soldier big as an Angus bull was kicking butt. He was a chocolate grizzly and fought like a drunken lumberjack. Nothing hurt him. He beat three Marines in one day, hitting their hardwood heads with fists tougher than the steel of axes. Then Red here fights the bull big enough to kick Charles Atlas around."

All within earshot on tent detail turned to listen.

"I can see that top Sergeant sitting Red down in

his corner. Then this Lieutenant comes out of a storeroom with Angus, holds up the ropes, ties the strings on his gloves and near as kisses him. What surprises me was the Lieutenant turns out to be Red's second." Christie's face reflected that surprise. "Top kick just sets a bottle in Red's corner, then leaves to go out in the seats to cover bets." Christie looked at me. "Sorry Red, I looked to make some money. No how I figured you to survive the first round when I see you without your fatigue shirt, a melting snowman to the other guy's pile of stones. So my money went down on Angus." Christie jumped to his feet, swinging at air, fighting a ghost. "Angus doesn't touch gloves at the bell. He shoots for teeth. Red is on his chest chopping. They swarm, lay all over, swing like two crazy men. It's a hell of a round." Christie knelt down. He wiped sweat from his brow. "When I hear Lieutenant doing a Cain on Abel telling Red to stay away from Angus and box, I know Red got Benedict Arnold in his corner. I figure to make real big money. Top covers me. The second round is colossal, savage, toe to toe." Christie was up, hitting with jabs and right crosses at air. "Angus breaks a clinch. Red stays on him like chest hair. Angus hollers 'come on and fight.' He misses a big shot at the bell."

    Christie was back on a knee, face red as the morning sun, eyes aglow. "Then Lieutenant takes to looking sickly when Red's blood drips on tailored fatigues. He tells Red he can't win on points. Red coughs his water across Lieutenant's crotch. Then I know that Lieutenant will toss the towel. Sorry Red," Christie said in apology, "I bet more on Angus. If Lieutenant is going to double-cross his own fighter, I want a cut." Christie wiped his brow. "At the bell Angus lunges broad as a courthouse door. Red's right catches his nose and it does old faithful. The bull comes on again swinging like a cattle gate. He loses all sense and takes a swipe at the referee, some drunken sergeant that backs into the ropes. Angus comes back at Red. It's another gusher when Red hits him square, like drilling for oil. Angus took to putting on a hell of a show falling against the ropes, bleeding on the referee, acting like a drunk. He backs off and looks at Red across the ring. What he saw was a bloody mess, welts on Red thick as bird droppings on mulberries! But believe it or not, Angus drops his gloves. He backs off. 'You a pro,' he says. 'Won't fight no pro.' He ups and quits and Lieutenant's still standing there with his towel."

    The squad took a long look at me, but said nothing.

BATTLE FOR THE OUTPOST

In charge of the 3rd section of machine guns was First Sergeant George Shoemaker, a soldier built like a pillar of concrete with chips knocked out for the eyes, nose, mouth and chin. He had his own intelligence system, far more reliable than the 'Stars and Stripes' newspaper. It centered around poker playing and stateside booze. Where Shoe got his booze was a closely held secret. Some one in Counter Intelligence (if any dared to visit a combat unit) might have suspected a breach of military secrecy because of Shoe's data gathering, save for his location: the Korean battlefront! He trod the dirt floors of Company Command Points, "CP" on the Main Line of Resistance, "MLR", even the wooden floors of Regimental tents in defense of his poker playing proficiency. Getting back to Division Rear wasn't beyond him! He was a sought after poker playing soldier with bottles of Stateside booze. Back there he got the latest 'word' from Division's War Tent's top enlisted men whose truce rumors were luminous as lightning bugs during mating season.

Shoe had the word 'Plan Overwhelming', the attack to Pyongyang and Wonsan had been shelved by General Van Fleet who doubted his replacement army could do it, drained as it was of its cream by rotation. Operation Talons went to the same shelf. It was to have been an advance ranging a mile in one place to fifteen miles in another to remove a sag in the line on the eastern front. Then, at September's end, an attack would have been launched in the west by the 25th Infantry Division attacking northeast followed by an amphibious landing on the east coast by the Marines attacking southwest. Their link up might have trapped innumerable enemy.

Shoe told us 'elbowing north', tidying the right flank, remained, but not the linkup. "Oddly," he said, "success of Talons might have caused the Chinks to lose too much face and thus jeopardize the truce talks!" To Shoe, the facts were plainly opposite. "Them Chinks only came to the negotiating table because so many of their comrades had their faces blown off by the Eight Army's spring and summer offensives. The termination of Talons has more to do with fear of the reaction to the GI casualty count. All hell will hit the fan back home where there was already a sense of futility about the fighting. Some sweet citizenry might be inconvenienced by the noises of politicians sounding off about a high casualty count. Don't know why Van Fleet's War Tent and our own home folks don't have the respect for us them Chinks have?"

In lieu of entering a truce, as Shoe told it, it was rumored the CCF might muscle flex by launching an attack to drive in the 35th RCT's 3rd Battalion outpost on hills 682 and 717. The 25th Infantry Division Headquarters, 'HQ' wasn't taking the rumor lightly. It wasn't unaware of the need to plug a penetration of the MLR in the event the high ground was taken by the Chinese. To counter, the whole of its infantry in every green valley and verdant mountain needed to be alert for the new moon of the autumnal season, for only then would its pale light be a jewel of guidance to a Chinese attack. Operations Plan No. 9 was readied. The 24th Regiment would secure the east shoulder of any penetration; the Turk Battalion assigned to the

25th Division the west shoulder; the 27th Regiment would block; while the 35th would counterattack to restore the frontline, line 'Wyoming'. Plan 'Operation Bump', would move and relocate the 35th's second battalion for this very purpose.

Shoemaker warned his section of machine guns that the patrol base of the 5th Cavalry regiment had been hit by two Chinese companies in a half circle around the base, supported by tanks. They had taken under fire a GI reinforcing patrol on the supply route to the patrol base. A battalion or more of Chinese had moved up. That wasn't all of it. The outpost of the 7th Infantry Division had been hit and overrun; the 1st Cavalry regiment's outpost had been driven in while the 3d Infantry Division's outpost had been brought under heavy attack.

Shoe pushed his squads to clean weapons and spare parts, check ammo, draw fresh water and combat rations while ranting, "no combat infantryman cared if he ever fired his weapon in a second fire fight, having survived the first. Yet, if war he must, an infantryman cared about the fire support he got after he crossed the line of departure, the 'LD'. He wants every weapon the Army and Air Force could fire will precede him, cover him, then follow up along with the men climbing the hill. An infantryman doesn't want limitation. He wants a choreography of shells, napalm and bullets dancing with him as his partner. It gives strength to legs heading into the enemy's trenches! If there's a battle, I want a big one. Spread them Chinks to their limits. Spread them so that a BAR can pin down a squad; a light thirty machine gun a platoon; Dog heavy thirties, a company. I don't want riflemen funneled in the sights of concentrated enemy fire and grenades. I don't want a limited war, freeing Chinks from some tunnel to reassemble at a hot spot. Them concentrated commies are like mowed dandelions; they regenerate by the hour."

Whatever Shoe's chatter, my squad leader, Staff Sergeant Dean Warren, a farmer built along the lines of a sturdy bull, wasn't too pleased the outpost's patrols came in without enemy contact or that Operation Bump moved the second battalion into counterattack positions. Warren was troubled that none of our troops had been placed on hill 432, the halfway point of the main supply route, 'MSR', between the Main Line of Resistance, 'MLR', and hills 682 and 717. No GIs on hill 432 meant it was open to an oriental express. If the Chinese hadn't gone over to defense in Kumhwa, but hit the 3d battalion of the 35th from the north, then swung behind the outpost to hill 432, the results were predictable. They'd made that maneuver elsewhere. The 1st Cavalry Division, the 7th and 3d Divisions all had their outposts hit just that way.

Did the Chinese think less of the 35th's eyes on its outpost? No! Love Company took thirty three rounds before 2012 hours when quiet prevailed until 0005 hours. Then, for twenty minutes, hills 717 and 682 were shelled before the CCF probed those positions. At 0115 hours, blowing bugles between the hills, they attacked, firing burp guns, hurling grenades, chanting.

The second battalion moved out at 0510 hours and into blocking as a part of Operation Bump. Fox Company formed up around Leader Baker's platoon of tanks from the 89th tank Battalion and deployed for attack to cross the Hantan River by a concrete bridge. King Company, traversing slopes in inky light, moved out over the MSR toward the outpost to reinforce the third battalion. But hill 432 was infested with Chinese soldiers well dug in between King and the outpost. The enemy laid down withering fire on the unsuspecting skirmish line; calling down heavy mortar rounds, pouring intense fire from automatic and small arms.

    The 14th Regiment was ordered to relief positions, freeing the 35th's 1st Battalion to prepare to attack on the right flank of 682; the 2nd battalion the left flank of 717. With this movement of massed forces, came a singular relocation. Sergeant Warren reposition his last ammo bearer to gunner of the squad's heavy machine gun. I, the first idiot, wondered "why me?" There were six other ammo bearers, and an assistant gunner with time in grade. A promotion? Or more to do with me being six feet two and the idiot that ran, to win a few beers, one hundred and twenty pounds of ammo up a steep hill? Or, I hoped not, Warren considered the others less expendable. Machine guns attracted incoming rounds like a latrine did flies. I was in the Army now, not in the seminary's library decks. Both places it was expected that orders were obeyed.

    While the machine gun section geared up, I heard King Company drove the Chinese off hill 432. To what avail? King was still catching lead up slope from hill 528. Too, like blows from a blacksmith's hammer, King's positions on 432 were shivered to splinters by incoming Chinese rounds. King was zeroed in. Not an inch uphill would be surrendered by the Chinese without killing, wounding or taking prisoners of everyone, or the destruction of the 3rd Battalion.

I worried for the men of Item, Love and Mike up on the outpost. They had taken fire all night. They'd expected reinforcements, but King was stymied by noon. The Chinese had slipped between the outpost and the front line, coming in by foot through the northeast valley between the Hantan River and the back end of the outpost. The move cut off GI resupply. It had been a silent envelopment. What King had intended - reinforcements - became a relief force.

The Chinese mission was one of destruction of an American Battalion, not a general attack. The Commies hadn't hit the MLR, but controlled the valleys through which the men of the 3rd battalion on the patrol base might withdraw, as well as holding back a reinforcing company. It was a well planned carp shoot!

GIs blamed the truce talks; our officers. Even if the talks were suspended, no one took it as final, just another stutter between inflammatory rhetoricians. Maybe our line officers were distracted, forgetting the mobility of the Chinese. A simple ounce of prevention - a patrol each night atop 432 - might well have prevented the Chinese infiltration. Too many of the Army's officers were educated and trained beyond the obvious. They couldn't see straight on. They saw the grand, the great picture, not the single Chinese in tennis shoes holding a burp gun in a fox hole on 432.

The 35th Raider platoon and the Turk Battalion moved out and secured the area by the concrete bridge. A forward aid station was set up. Helicopters evacuated the wounded from Chongyon-ni. Fox Company and Northstar tanks jumped off at 1410 hours to backstop King on 432. King moved out against 528. A platoon of George Company and a tank platoon moved into the valley to break through. There was no doubt that Item, Love and Mike were encircled.

None of us in the 1st Battalion would be of mortal coil if we'd not felt the wrong done to the 3rd battalion - the Blue battalion, (the 1st, the Red Battalion, the 2nd, the White), their endangerment inflicted by friendly thoughtlessness, their wounds by the enemy.

I felt more than queasiness in my stomach at the thought that the battalion wasn't looking for Chinese, but for GIs trapped by the Chinese. I sensed an onset of diarrhea! Bad water I'd heard, but I drank only GI water from the water bag. At that, I touched up each canteen of water with a halazone tablet. Not a drop of the natural fluid in mountain streams had passed my lips, yet my innards were in convulsion. If it weren't the water, might it have been the c-ration of canned meat called hamburgers that looked like sheet metal cemented between lubricant? Even heated over my mobile cook stove they tasted like axle grease off a Conestoga wagon wheel. How could I go into combat with fatigues full of effluvium? I smiled at the thought I'd fill them anyway at the first impact of the enemy's incoming shells. Our tiny Missouri medic, Corporal Wilbur 'Doc' Davidson, had a cure for it. "Bowel plug," he called it, a sip or two taken every few hours. It would bind whatever needed binding; loosen what needed loosening.

"Hear the word," Shoe yelled. The rotation of

his shoulders diverted attention to his helmet's lip fringed by long blond bangs, self cut, like Moe of the three Stooges had barbered. "Trucks will move us at 1800 hours. Red Lynx will relieve us."

"Who be Red Lynx," inquired Private Earl Diemer, a scarecrow in uniform, the section's untidiest soldier. This time, however, his weapon, cartridge belt and pack straps were clean, pack squared. He was as sharp as if a joint venture of janitorial firms had taken him under contract.

Private Im Ta Song had done the cleaning. He was a Korean soldier assigned to the US Army. 'KATUSA', as they were know in official circles. To us GIs, he was Joe ROK. His big brown eyes were turned on like lanterns at the spectacle of Diemer, so different from other Americans. Joe ROK had told me he believed Diemer must have been sold to an American Yangban family. When in olden times Korean parents found they could no longer provide for their children they sold them to preserve their lives, and their parents'. Children of such slaves were also slaves and compelled to serve the same master as their parents had served. Slaves could never escape from their recorded social status. They were branded for life. They were, even in death, carried behind a red mourning banner inscribed with the words 'private servant's coffin'. Slavery had been abolished in Korea in 1894, but the GI ammo bearer Diemer hadn't escaped his social status.

Shoe choked on his swallow of tobacco. He saw a miraculous apparition in the form of the not-moldy Diemer. The section sergeant patooied a wad through open tent flaps. Clearing his throat, he said, "Red Lynx is the first battalion, 14th Regiment. Red Leopard is us, Diemer, the 1st battalion of the 35th. We're moving up. Saddle up!"

I swung the tripod to my shoulders, (the machine gun would later be mounted on it), and clomped a hand onto a thrust out forward leg. I said a short prayer for safety. There followed a sinking sensation. Innards roiled and we were just to leave for the assembly area. Was my courage fleeing? An uncomfortably moist sensation ran between my shoulder blades. I hoped it was sweat, not a dented beer can leaking.

"Move out!" Shoe ordered.

I followed Sergeant Warren down the slow incline. Tailing us were Private Hartland Clouse, Assistant Gunner. He carried the machine gun. Private William Bouton, 1st Ammo Bearer carried the weapon's water can and a can of ammo. Each of the ammo bearers of the 1st gun carried two cans of ammo. The 2nd gun squad followed the 1st. We snaked downhill in a bold front. I felt a plaintive breeze that wafted parting sighs toward the son of Irish immigrants and men descended from America's immigrant Poles, Frenchmen, Germans, Englishmen, central Europeans. Crafty Shoemaker, methodical Doc Davidson, the caring Iowa farmer Warren, sinful Clouse of Pennsylvania, soulful Bouton, religious Carroll Truscott, argumentative Norbert Gzregorek, slim witted Earl Diemer, hysterical Baldy Heideman, Bayou Boudreau and puzzling Joe ROK - men, armed and dangerous, going to battle as ordered, but not before verbalizing dejectedly on the blood lines coursing through the veins of military planners.

We mounted two and a half ton trucks. They roared off. Fine dust off the road powdered the section. Some coughed. No one complained. It was a ride, not a march. It might have been over smoother roads but Korea had no Main Street. Sudden stops and starts had backsides sliding. Fatigues were proving non-splinter proof. Trepidation was my relative. I swigged bowel plug and squirmed from cheek to cheek.

A jerky stop stacked us like dominoes. It shook loose my sphincter. At the stop, I leapt from the stalled convoy like a deer from a hunter, hitting the grounds with legs hastening me into a bushy ravine. Mission accomplished, I ambled back as if returning to a ride in a hay wagon. Remounted, I slurped more gastrointestinal stopper.

"The runs be like on a roller coaster, Red," Diemer said. "When you be rumbling all over, you know you ain't being done right. When it's over you know you been somewhere."

The truck turned wheels again, jolting, jerking, shifting the troops in all directions. I felt compelled to do something to soothe jangled emotions and hurting hind-end. I had a tendency to sing, mostly to myself in the gun or sleeping bunkers. Sometimes I sang a popular song, but now, riding to battle, the urge to chant as if back in the seminary came to mind. What better than a prayer!

"Our Father, Who art in heaven, hallowed be thy name, thy kingdom come, thy will be done on earth as it is in heaven.

Give us this day our daily bread, and forgive us our trespasses as we forgive those who trespass against us, and lead us not into temptation, but deliver us from evil."

I stressed the words 'deliver us from evil' increasing the volume that the Good Lord hear and give us His protection.

I wasn't sure what Sergeant Warren responded, but it sounded prayerful.

The truck convoy burped its way forward over trails bulldozed through skinned slopes still bleeding clots of stone. The wheeled snake expanded and contracted like an anaconda beneath ridge lines pointing mean fingers at each deuce and a half ton truck passing by benevolently. I tried not to listen to the truck cab's canvas roof flapping up and down like a quacking duck. I studied the hills. I saw dull ridge lines with grotesque humpback and pimple peaks wounded by jagged trench lines still catching fading sunlight with haze from cordite clouds swirling above moonscape heights. There was little greenery left between rival armies. Soldiers weren't issued green thumbs. The tools of their trade turned verdure to sable, cooked by military volcanoes - napalm and white phosphorus. My eyes were witnessing the soot of combat.

The convoy jerked to a stop. I leapt off the truck and flashed the sprinting style of the hundred yard dasher along the roadside beside the line of idling trucks. The bestial turns my innards took was if six butchers were twisting my guts to make sausage. Behind the bush, my convulsions were cheers. I shivered despite the warm evening. Then a leg cramped came. Its pain was second to none. I pushed up from my haunches to let blood course through veins. Then I felt an unearthly fire in my eyes, worse than the leg cramp when I recognized the unmistakable shape of a mine field sign. I was within its boundaries! "Oh Lord!"

How did I get out? My buddies in the deuce-by offered naught but warnings. There wasn't walking out as I'd run in. I pulled up my fatigue pants and tightened the belt buckle. I clicked closed my cartridge belt and felt for my bayonet. I'd have to probe for mines with it. We'd trained that way in basic.

"That's it," Warren yelled. "Be careful!"

'Careful' became my first, middle and surname. I bent from the waist, feet firmly fixed, and probed a semi-circle. No metallic contact. I slowly dropped to hands and knees. Prayer became a closer companion than it had any of my five years in the seminary. Perhaps all seminarians should do combat time to truly feel what's behind a request to God. My bayonet gently probed an arc of ground. Clear. I probed and crawled, probed and crawled an arc at a time, obsessed I'd never crap again. One didn't have to in heaven. Right?

"There's ten yards to go, Red," Warren shouted. "Just keep probing and crawling."

A metallic click rippled the air as loudly as a sentry's safety when released to challenge a suspected enemy. The sound of my bayonet against a rock or a land mine? If a rock, I worried my quivering might set off another of the deadly things. I marked the location with sticks. I probed left, nothing there, then angled back toward Warren, finding soft clay an arc at a time to the warning sign. Crawling out of the mine field summoned the last particle of spent nerves. My pasty face harbored every fugitive freckle passed through to me from eight hundred years of Irish ancestry and prior centuries of Celtic genes in Wales.

"You looked a prehistoric snail creeping an inch a minute, Red," Warren said. "Lucky it's not your time." The look on his face, relived, leaned more to disgust at my stupidity.

Shoe's manner of speech couldn't be described as relief he'd not lost a gunner, especially the suggested treatment for my loosened bowels - a carbine up my rectum. Every time he spoke, hollered that was, the scar on his chin grew white at the edges, matching the color of his huge eyebrows. Yet, there was a tinge of fluff in his sound. No GI wanted to see a soldier blown apart in a mine field.

I got back on the truck to stay there, no matter if my infirmity back flushed out my throat. Too soon we disembarked and assembled. I looked around. Nothing, from rock to rock, hill to hill, looked familiar to the contours on a map. Was one or the other of the close high hills 717, 682? I clung closely to Warren, following him down a deep ravine. A cup of hot soup would have done me right to offset an internal chill. It was a misery of a day. I sweated; I shivered in sweat soaked fatigues; my bowels twisted me green. I worried there was dust in the machine gun and ammo belts that needed removal while noting my innards were churning bowel plug to cement. A break from the march was ordered. I flipped the tripod to ground and sat down on a rock.

Shoemaker set out the order of attack to his squads. "Baker Company's point squad will move out in a diamond to hill 432 with a connecting file back to the advance platoon, then the rest of Baker comes up. Charley, Dog and Able companies follow in a column of twos maintaining tactical unity. Each man holds to a distance of two paces between them as it darkens."

Reflections of searchlights probing the clouds exposed hundreds of GIs in the valley. Some cleaned weapons. Others stood tall, leaning on rifles. A few sat Indian style, weapons across their knees. No one smoked. Few talked. Someone, from out of the dark, gave the order to saddle up and up came the tide of troops, orderly, in no hurry. Baker formed up and moved out. An exodus of men went into the inky recesses of ravines and slopes as wrinkled as Oliver Hardy's waistline. Boots trampled through the lowering dark.

"Hear the word," shouted Shoe. "We're done farting around waiting for truce talks to do something. We've had enough of them Chinks on our outpost. We're going up there and circumcise the lot. First we're going up to hill 432 and dig in. Then we're going to cross a valley and go up that ridge line as quick-like as Red running to take a crap. We're going to bust through!" He clamored in cheer leader tone, wanting his men fired up. He wanted spirit. They had climbed those torturously twisted uphill ridges a few weeks back when the outpost, now bald as a baby's butt, was first taken. Back then it was humidity undulating out of the valley. Now it would be heat from Chinese mortars. "The long sit down is over! To hell with the fiction of a demarcation line and a cease fire," Shoe said, putting ferocity into his sound. "We'll take it to the Chinks! You hear, squad leaders. I want a conversation out there, gunners! I want your guns talking, bursts so synchronized the Chinks will look for one weapon." He slipped a grenade onto each of his pack strap loops. His cartridge belt carried extra magazine pouches. He shouldered his carbine. His helmet was pitched at bushy eyebrow height. "Saddle up! Move out!"

Behind the broad tree trunk of the section sergeant stepped the thickset Iowan as if off to the back eighty acres to hand husk corn from stalks. I marveled that men going to battle would stride forth vigorously as if on a pilgrimage to Canterbury. The rest of the section was quiet, but quiet was fire in the heart. I sensed adrenaline rising. They would not let the lives of the 3rd battalion, or ours, be thrown away.

The enemy was alive and well and in these hills. It wasn't training. I was no longer moving with impunity. A mortar round smacked forward. I questioned if I'd stripped down to essentials: a pencil, notebook, camera, film, toothbrush, shaving brush, soap, a brush for the weapon, three beers, extra socks. Toilet paper? I carried enough if the bowel plug slowed the propulsive waves within the intestinal tract!

I moved carefully over the rock strewn ridge worried that there might not be fox holes on 432, that mortars might catch the 1st gun squad digging in. My carbine rode Warren's left shoulder. My back pack carried a set of spare parts - a lock frame, bolt and barrel extension, extra packing for the muzzle gland and muzzle end. Three cans of combat rations were tucked inside clean socks to avoid rattling. A termite grenade rode the loop of my left pack harness to use on the machine gun if over run. That was an image my fantasy hadn't yet constructed. Carbine ammo clips hung on the cartridge belt with a canteen, first aid packet and entrenching tool. A fragmentary grenade rode the loop of the right pack harness.

Once in a while, somewhere in the vast darkness, a pocket of resistance erupted, the long column halted, a squad sent around the pocket to envelope the blockage. Suddenly the column moved again! I welcomed the respites. Tripods, machine guns, weapons might be lowered, a quick breath taken before the oft repeated orders to saddle up and move out again.

The wreckage of past fire fights was strewn all along the ridges: ammo boxes, expended clips, canteens, a broken weapon, brass from expended rounds. Salvage was the chore of others. Infantrymen were the makers of waste, human or manufactured. We kept on the move across this desolate debris, under hissing white flares falling from the heavens that threw momentary garish light. I was awe struck to be a part of it.

"Take ten," Shoemaker directed. He was uneasy. He told us the truth, as he knew it, of the situation facing the outfit in the hazy distance, beyond the dim horizon on nature's fort of hills 682 and 717. "The remnants of the 3rd battalion plus Fox were dug in up there last night," he pointed toward hill 432, a vague peak beneath the shades of night. "No friendly sharks could move because of the box mines so Blue three and twelve GIs had to hole up over night at Tanwon-ni. They got back to the MLR. Sixty-eight more came in later. Both the 24th and 27th Regiments have pulled in their outposts. This may be the beginning of the Chinks' seventh phase offensive."

"Why the hell are we moving up," the startled Warren questioned?

"There's still a lot of GI's unaccounted for," Shoe said. "They may still be alive up there.

Blue Six took a chance that few, if any, of his men were on hill 528. He cleared the order to fire across its crest and on its north side."

I perceived agony in the decision. The crushing crescendo of the thundering shells, the angry shock waves that stirred the still air to a tempest, the trembling of the very earth as if the god of volcanoes had come home, was not lightly called in where friendly troops might be.

Shoe had more to say, "George Company ran recon patrols all night beyond the perimeter of 432 to pick up friendly wounded and stragglers. Instead they took fire from Chinks all over the place looking for prisoners. The Chinks aren't pulling out. They're dug in on 528 and patrolling. They hold the outpost. It's still anyone's guess if they're going to hit the MLR. They've changed their strategy. They're standing still and fighting for ground. The Blue boys fought all night at Tanwon-ni. Enemy fire came in like a tropical rain. Damned if they didn't shoot our own weapons at us. GI ammo was too low to answer round for round, but they told me our artillery built a wall around them. It even looked as if the Chinks would pay any price to drive Fox Company off of 432. Chinks crept up to within yards of the perimeter. Pay they did. Fox and King were set for all around defense - had a lot of ammo and grenades. They were buttoned up. In came a heavy volley of rifle and burp gun fire; the enemy walking straight in, firing as they came. Their mortar men came up too, belching 57 millimeter rounds into Fox even though the enemy's night cover had been penetrated by the flickering of yellow gold flares and searchlights beams bouncing off low passing clouds. Scores of hunched enemy flowed down from hill 528. Fox's men thickened the air with lead. Their mortar men fed their tubes until they were red hot. Artillery danced shells from 432 up the ridgeline." His words were painting a playwright's scene as if Shoe's men were viewing the firestorm on stage. "GI grenades perforated quilted cotton pants like so many needles. Heavy machine guns crackled blue, white and red streams of flame across the Chink skirmishers dueling with the enemy's automatic weaponry. It hadn't been a long fire fight, but the never ceasing cannonading of the 89th artillery battalion made it seem forever. Their bone shattering shells walked the ridges up to hill 528, chopping remnants of crimson commies like weeds."

    I wished Shoe's story had been a mere baseball game played for a winner's share of spectator's money. I would never again enjoy the artificial suspense created by a pitcher holding a one run lead and a runner on third with the bases loaded, two outs in the bottom of the ninth of the world series, a two strike, three ball count on the batter. Such was mere psychological hysteria. Death didn't ride on the outcome.

    "Fox deployed a platoon," Shoe said. "It moved forward on hill 528 firing at targets of opportunity. A BAR-man went down from a bullet. His ammo bearer exchanged his rifle for the BAR, called the medic, then stood to fire a burst in anger. His churning mind must have driven him forward. He fired as he marched into an incoming burst. Riflemen to the left of the formation fell, their buddies hesitating only to drag the wounded behind rock cover, calling the medic, then moving up the hill in the skirmish line. They moved up the ridgeline like a sickle. Their lieutenant's hollering was stilled by a bullet, but they were a well-trained rifle outfit. They rallied behind the voice of their platoon sergeant. He moved the remnants of his four squads forward a hundred feet before he fell to a slug. Then the senior squad leader took over. The fire was so fierce, he ordered his men to take cover. When Fox Six offered the senior squad leader a fresh platoon, the offer was rejected. His men would conquer the crest. It was their mission. They would complete it. Bayonets were fixed. Fresh platoons were deployed to lay down overhead cover. A strange new energy flowed into every muscle of those men. They told the covering platoons not to shift fire before they saw the attackers actually in enemy trenches. Then they charged up the hill like Civil War cavalry. Their bayonets swept the crest of hill 528 just like they did last February on hill 440." Shoe crushed his fists into his eyes, but issued an order. "Saddle up!" A moment later, "Move out!"

  We climbed hill 432 and took cover. The fighting hole left behind by other soldiers fitted me and assistant gunner Clouse too tightly. I wished my helmet was as large as Mom's wash tub. Why had the metallurgists of an infantryman's head armor formed tooled steel not much larger than a coffee cup? I wanted a helmet along the lines of a cast iron bathtub. There might not be much sense in a brain that volunteered its body for combat in Korea, but whatever the amount of gray matter that resided between the occipital and parietal bones, I didn't want scattered across the rock strewn earth of the mountains north of Kumhwa.

"Never can get deep enough in a gun hole," said Clouse. He lost little time in getting to work enlarging the position. He dug as quietly, the entrenching tool under control, as if looking for truffles. Every minute he expected a burp gun to open up. Cold shivers crawled his back each time I raised a striking noise off a rock. Under his breath, he cursed my recklessness. He motioned for less forceful digging. When a parachute flare sparkled its garishness, he froze in place until the darkness returned. When the hole reached an acceptable depth, he stopped digging and rolled up like a catatonic in a sit down fetal grip. "Take two sand bags out of my pack, Red."

His helmet fit his head like a diver's bell. I began to doubt the assertion that steel pots were all of the same size, that the helmet liner inside the helmet might be adjusted to any size head - fat or thin! How could one soldier wear a helmet turtle-like, while another looked to be wearing no more than a thimble around his temples? It was a matter I'd check into back at Company. In the meanwhile, I freed two floppy sack's from Clouse's pack. "Why are you carrying sand bags?"

"For sand!" he moaned, his child like cheeks and razor thin lips puckering in exasperation to remonstrate the silly questioner. "For sand," he repeated, "if there is any sand or dirt on this forsaken pile of rocks." His head slumped, the nape of his grimy neck between the break of his fatigue shirt and rear helmet lip his only epidermis exposed to his foxhole buddy. "Fill 'em up. Put them either side of the gun so our heads got cover if it's a fire fight."

It was a veteran's trick of the trade. Corporal Habjanitz, my predecessor gunner, wouldn't have expected less. He would have known Korea might be a country fortified by nature, but an entrenching tool and sand bags were soldiers' tools to fortify defensible space. If a gun crew was to come back off a hill unaided, they needed to dig in and lay sand bags against a flood of lead, high pitched bravado and the screech of bugles. Sand bags absorbed shredded lead like breakfast oats did milk. I credited Clouse as a soldier of purpose, although a bit high strung. With two women back home alleging paternity suits, perhaps that was why he sat mostly comatose in the gun hole. I let the slight fellow alone, knowing he would recoup his fortitude, if that was what he had left Stateside.

I took over, lessening grains' fierce grip from the soil's thin veneer. There must have been vegetation once upon a time, not just weathering rocks, over which organic materials grasped tenuous footholds. Through the centuries, rock was transformed to soil, but not much up this hill in Korea; just enough for two sand bags full. They took places of honor either side of the bullet spitting weapon, to shield eyes above gun hole rampart left behind by Fox and George Companies.

Up beyond hill 528, I watched the explosive flashes of friendly artillery fire walk the ridge line north through the trench lines of the Chinese, clear up to hills 682 and 717. It was answered in kind. Mortar fire walked the ridgelines of hill 528. I saw a fearsome place where infantry curled like worms and burrowed ever deeper into the trembling earth. Survival was in a deep narrow hole.

    Fox and George left more than their excavations. They left trepidation; cordite as thick as a milk shake; extinguished Chinese laying about the slopes in weird, contorted poses. I was shocked at what artillery could do to flesh and bones, mangling and slaughtering men who moments before were bearers of intellects. The scene was appalling. Dreadful specters, their wretched legs hanging from tissue. There were appalling clumps of dissected limbs; guillotined heads; separated hands more claws than the agile digits they had been but hours before. Vacant stares locked a last view within decomposing bodies. I'd seen Movie Shows of the like, but not with guts, arms and legs loose as spaghetti drenched in tomato sauce.

    The stench of the dead hung over hill 432 like a sordid cloud, its fetid stink blending with cordite, an odor of diarrhea, gangrene, violent straining, clots of blood, vomit, mucus, discharged blood blotches. The odor was the sickly reek of decaying, putrefying flesh unable to be buried while the living yet fought deadly battles throughout a ghostly night and glum days.

    My blood chilled at the sight of rats down the hill, going from corpse to corpse, running over bodies, foraging for food, chewing at faces, eating human meat! I shuddered. Those destructive, elongated, virtually invisible black mammals hissed like rattlesnakes.

    I'd been instructed during basic training to hate

the enemy. The decimation of a foe that sought to mangle or kill Americans in the 3rd battalion was a quid pro quo. Chinese were the enemy. It was kill and not be killed! Both ways! The dismal darkness and the gloomy dead were evidence that war was extirpation of infantrymen by bits and pieces, with the soldiers of China littering hill 432. My grim thoughts weren't heartless, merely professional. They had attacked during the truce talk lull, with scorn on their mind, fire in their weapons, to beat back the outposts of a quiet army! They'd asked for it! Why? Probably because I now concluded the Chinese sought truce talks only to reorganize their armed manhood for reconstituted combat tactics formulated on the Soviet Union's theories of battle. No matter the motives of the Commies' commanders, I prayed for the souls of the Chinese carcasses spread over the hillside.

There were still two hours of guard duty to pull before crossing the morning's LD. The pangs of a bodily craving roiled. I was famished. It had been a blind grab of rations before mounting the trucks, and with chow time curtailed by sprints to the latrines in response to the explosive tendencies of entrails, and the dig for land mines, I hadn't eaten. I couldn't eat captured on the back bench of a 2x2 truck in a dusty convoy. I couldn't eat while on the long slow climb from the jump off point to the crest of hill 432. The gloomy and gaunt desolation of night guard and night combat turned my monitor from amino acids to animal survival. But at last the time to chow down arrived. I freed a circular, inch and a half deep can from my pack, then took hold of the can opener on my dog tag chain to open the lid of the morsel. The light of a flickering flare revealed the ration to be cheese and bacon. It was what Doc Davidson would have prescribed as a sequel to the original treatment for loose bowels, even though my intestines already must have been coated to a chalky goo. I rummaged through the pack for a substitute meal. Darn! All three of my combat rations were cheese and bacon! I gave entertainment to waking Clouse, but thought better of it. A breakfast of cheese and bacon wasn't all bad. It would certainly cork! A surety for the swigging of Doc's denominated 'bowel plug'. If it were cheese and bacon for breakfast, no less than a beer was needed to wash it down. The tiny sharp point of the can opener ate into the can top with the force of a tooth twisting. The cheese was congealed into a miniature wheel. If the label hadn't defined the dark particles interspersed throughout the yellowish substance as bacon, I might have concluded the cheese packing plant had included high protein flies. The cheese wheel was too thick for the all purpose spoon. So I nibbled edges, oblivious to salivating rodents.

What would Dad think of his ex-seminarian if he knew his lad was in no-man's land poised to attack and retake the Regiment's outpost? Dad and Mom would be in church, not praying for themselves, but for my safety, praying for a truce. If it was Sunday, Dad's men's choir, like a concert of harps and his tuba base would be singing four part harmony at the Latin High Mass. In silent delight, the distant son heard the music.

"Saddle up," hollered Shoe.

I cleared the steam tube and web belt from the machine gun before waking Clouse. Bouton, our first ammo bearer, came over from his foxhole and took away the water can and can of ammo. I pulled the rear locking pin out, and Clouse removed the front locking pin and lifted the gun from the mount rotating the weapon to his left shoulder. He looked a little boy with a toy cannon. I stood up and swung the tripod to my shoulders and said a prayer.

"1st gun," whispered the hoarse Warren, "come to the reverse slope, here!" He motioned Ammo bearer Diemer to a low profile.

The squalid soldier was walking as upright as a garbage man to a picnic. Whatever had happened to his earlier cleanliness was beyond comprehension. At least the ammo cans he carried were latched closed, hopefully protecting the belt from taint. I visualized the head of the local draft board slinking around the corner after getting Diemer enrolled. So must have done the Army medical doctor who declared the rancid guy physically fit; the felony compounded by basic training company cadre that graduated the mold after sixteen weeks of rifle and heavy weapons training. Everyone stateside must have thought it better that Diemer, not them, ship out.

"Squad column," Warren ordered.

He watched us form. I stood first before him. Clouse was five yards across, and five back. Five yards behind me knelt Bouton, then at five yard intervals across and back were Truscott, Heideman, Gzregorek, Boudreau and Diemer, all standing mast tall, then Joe ROK, squatting Korean style, like simulating taking a dump. The 2nd gun squad formed up behind us.

Shoemaker made his squads take the lowest profile possible. If there was a hole, we got into it until his order to move out was given. He had his way. If there were no holes, we hit the prone, stayed low and laid by our weapons and gear, ever ready to dig dirt! "You got ta' be quick or you're gonna be dead,' he lectured. "Most of you ain't been on an attack, but we've trained ya'. Do what I and the squad leaders tell ya' to do!" He spat chewing tobacco while studying us. Few were old timers. His machine-gun section had been filled out with replacements, most of whom had arrived after Operation Piledriver ended. The real combat infantrymen, so we were often told, had gone home since June 14. Those guys had driven north thirty-seven miles in ten days from May 21 to the 31st. Then they jumped off on June 3 on Piledriver. We'd heard the Chinese fought like hell, their rear guards on every hill around the roads of Chorwon and Kumhwa. It was a cock fight to reach line Wyoming, but the 35th Regiment had! What the aid stations and grave registration hadn't collected, rotation had!

    No question Shoe had as many doubts about us as turtles in from the sea had eggs to lay in the sand. We had more than a thousand meters to attack across. There were crevices, ravines, slopes, ridgelines, peaks, crests, and cliffs to climb in hot muggy weather; and every meter zeroed in by Chinese mortars and artillery, not to minimize automatic weapons and small arms.

    "Hear the word," called Shoemaker.

    I marveled at the poise of my section sergeant. He pushed up the peak of his helmet. The wide expanse of his blond creepy eyebrows wiggled in the light, eyes sparkling as if a military offensive was appetite satisfying. His smiling mouth flashed a cord of teeth stacked above the pillow of his chin. He was smiling at combat. What tremendous courage to not only open the gate of hell, but to lead his Dog heavies across it's blazing coals. As if a deadly cloud flowed out of that gate, I swore I saw crimson in the misty distance. Was it a vision? A hallucination?

"Hear the word," Shoe repeated. "Baker Company will cross the LD at 0600 hours," he checked his wrist watch," in two minutes. Charley Company follows, then Able Company. When Baker takes check point sixteen, Charley leapfrogs through to take check point thirty-five, then in attack echelon, Charley's 3rd platoon moves out to take the outpost. We go up with them, attached to Sergeant Smith's 3rd squad." The order came: "Move out." Right arm swinging forward, index finger pointing north, Shoe stepped out.

Our 3rd section's 1st and 2nd guns tied in to Charley Company's 3rd platoon echeloned to the right. Charley's 1st, 2nd and weapons platoon, (light machine guns and 61 millimeter mortars), moved in platoon columns, a rifle squad on the point in a diamond formation that connected with Baker's reserve platoon.

Nothing was going easily. Winds sighed in the thick brush on the lower slopes. I saw weary clouds stray and discovered the hillsides of the morning were as rough and uneven as were those of last night. Heaps of stones were loosened by clomping combat boots. Freed stones careened down washes cut over decades by torrents. I saw shell bursts had branded tree trunks where my outfit was yet to march. Branches were shivered, roots castrated. I calculated the rumblings of artillery behind me, their explosions ahead, were acting as sky borne sweepers clearing Chinese mine fields. At least I hoped so.

Coming down hill, a fertile green valley opened before my eyes, the valley's distant head quite wide but terraced as if an immense amphitheater had been cut below frowning cliffs. The broad flat floor at the close end was two football lengths between knife like ridges. It had to be crossed! There was an abundance of cover on the lower slopes as opposed to the egg head baldness of the peaks where battle might be fought for the high ground. Baker Company had just crossed these lower lands between desolate tentacles curving down from the outpost. Charley Company was next.

The valleys which laid athwart or sloped away from their promontories had been little altered by the guns of war, the winds or the weather, as far as I could determine. They were mindful of those my father told of that beautified his boyhood home in Country Antrim, Ireland, the opposite end of the globe from Korea. I remembered his description: green hills as round as soccer balls that swept down toward the little town of Loughguile, and echoed to the bleating of many sheep on its hillsides. Dad had told of the hazel nut copse, the wild raspberry bed, a red rowan tree, as if he were in God's garden.

Suddenly, Chinese in blocking positions ensconced in rock wall crevices, let loose a harassing fire, shooting down at the approaching men of Charley and Dog, taking Charley Company's point squad under fire, cutting them off from Baker Company. Smith's squad deployed and returned fire. Its BAR man sprayed the successive steps of the ascent through the hard wood and scrub forest that was dressed in green on the lower fingers up to the high side scarred ridgelines. Charley's light machine guns overrode the BAR across the low dips to their front. The company had scant cover of leafy vegetation against the flailing lead of undetected enemy. The light machine guns weren't defrocking the enemy's cloak.

"Dog heavies," called Smith.

Tying into Baker was imperative. There was to be no more encirclement. Getting up the hill to the checkpoint was the key to the plan of attack. Side by side, attacking battalions would eliminate flanking fire and free the 3rd battalion from the jaws of an entrapment.

"We're on the way, Smithy," answered Shoe.

Smith's 3rd squad of riflemen was pinned down. Under the strain from an imminent truce, even old timers like Smith, Shoemaker and Warren were beginning to show rust. It must have bothered Smith, as it did Shoe, to preside over the dispatch of 3rd squad's and 3rd section's nearly green troops against Chinese veterans. Yet, Smith must have wondered where the wells of courage and duty were back in America of which Shoe's soldiers coming forward had imbibed.

Warren was on us as if back at crew drill. He had confidence in us, watching as Clouse and I put the weapon into action with precision and speed. Exactness of squad teamwork in the rear was replicated on the grassy field. I took a sitting position silhouetted as if for a portrait, head erect, eyes to the front. On command, my tracers chewed paths through flora and fauna up suspect crevices, across fingers, into dark black holes.

Sergeant Smith deployed his squad. Charley Company moved across the valley and fanned out through the foliage to engage and suppress any remaining islands of resistance.

"Cease fire," ordered Shoe.

The echo of Dog thirties played the distant amphitheater as our machine guns went out of action when a sniper's round whumped earth. In the instant it took the sniper to sight and squeeze off another round, all of the machine gun section wallowed in beds of grass and weeds, indistinguishable from any other lump in the tall shoots of wild growth in the untended pasture.

Sergeant Smith organized his squad for a sweep of the lower slopes. The light machine guns were called for cover and played a concert for the sniper.

"Saddle up," Shoe called. "Move out!"

Moving up the steep incline toward the checkpoint, it was beyond the scope of my imagination to conceive that other human beings would call mountain climbing fun. If the officers had enlisted men climb mountains, obviously no fun was intended. On the shoulders of the peaks above me, there were piles of naked rocks. The outpost filled the sky on the north, a long ridge that ran the west sky. Faint white puffs floated by. Whether they were nature's clouds or the military's vapors, I couldn't discern. What I did see through the wild foliage of still leafy trees or the side slopes, was the edge of a mighty precipice. It marked a cleft stone, and a sharp upward turn to our climbing. It was a tortuous journey that a mountain goat wouldn't take, but we, soldiers under orders, dispossessed of mental faculties, did. Nature's charms, if this part of

Kumhwa had any, were being hideously despoiled by booted feet seeking footings. Stragglers lagged far down the mountain side. There was no path to follow, save the beaten trail crushed into the soil by the GIs who had gone on before. Exhausted men dispersed to seek easier ways, to blaze trails of their own. The mountain was testing the limitations of America's foot soldiers.

Breasting the long ascent was a group of more savage peaks than I could have dreamt possible. Still ahead of us were two thousand yards to reach check point thirty five and beyond that, the right flank of the outpost. Its solitude was being desecrated and shaken by perpetual out going rounds, belching the lives they devoured.

Clouse, Bouton and I used feet, knees, fingernails, teeth to grab hold to get our equipment up hill one foot at a time. I pulled myself, by now a limp rag, to the check point position, then tumbled onto the reverse slope's inhospitable stones. It had taken six morning hours to climb to a peak that pierced shadowy clouds. Even the wind up that high was weary.

I uncapped my canteen.

"Water on a ridgeline is blood to a living body, Red," said Clouse. "Sip."

I sipped. Downward on the deep lengthy slope, I saw steam escape from water cooled bodies as stragglers inched their way to the crest. Troops were strung out like boxer's teeth. Tactical unity hung in the balance. Radiomen, mortarmen, recoilless rifle squads, the 1st gun squad's ammo bearers, the 2nd gun squad, riflemen and chogie bearers were slow to assemble on the check point. The fortunes of war luckily found an absence of Chinese on the high ground of check point sixteen.

No sooner assembled than the order was given by Shoe, "Move out."

I shivered. Had I but one more minute to live? My guts felt as if a horse had kicked them. I diagnosed it as gastrointestinal. All that bacon and cheese! I calculated my intestines had turned to granite. My hands held the tripod in a death vise grip. I prayed as our big guns opened up, shells swooshing above. Thunderous blasts snorted ahead. A chugging round rent the air; its bits of shrapnel spider webbing the sky. The uneven ridgeline hadn't yet been denuded by human or insect encroachment. Mountain pines climbed the hill from the stream below up over the thousand foot ridge. There were white pines, quite tall, and quite out of reach of any villagers who had lived in the valleys. Some trees looked like balsam firs, others, junipers of ancient years still crouching and stubbornly clinging. They bore picturesque gnarled branches. Some were beautifully decorated by nature with tufts of gray-green leaves. A patch of larches gave witness to past limitations on timbering. I remembered Dad, a master carpenter, telling tall larches had heavy, hard, strong, dense and durable wood that took a brilliant polish. Yet, I wasn't walking in a sylvan botanical arboretum but under a pall that shadowed yesterday's casualties.

My first glimpse of dead GIs caused more surprise than sorrow. I knew GIs were as likely to die in battle as was the enemy, but I hadn't ever seen a dead GI. Here were a half dozen laid side by side. They could have been in a funeral parlor, so neatly arranged were they. None had limbs missing. Their bodies were still in full field dress. Bodies that once were full of vigor were waxen, pale of face and hands, blood spots staining their fatigues. A lone rifleman guarded them. He could have been at prayer the way he knelt over them. I let loose a prayer of my own for the repose of their souls with God this moment.

There was little grandeur in the stillness of corpses. Although their families would be regretfully told of their honorable demise, there still would be pain and despair in the zone of the interior. The beauty in fall's leaves of orange and gold would be overshadowed by the bleakness of the military grave. Families would weep over lost loves. Their faces and forms would reappear in the picture shows of their mothers' and fathers' memories until recollection was but a last snapshot taken the day they shipped out to Korea.

Why did the sight of dead GIs stir so? Because the vague fear I had of the terrible consequences of war had become manifest. There followed the recognition life lived in combat could be very brief. I felt mortal, not helpless, never hopeless, just fragile. It was an enervating sensation. I controlled it.

My cognitive processes prior to this view had focused on the high death toll of Chinamen, not friendly casualties, as ironic a phrase as the Army could invent. Here were Americans killed in action, 'KIA.' Did the abbreviation glorify these faithfully military departed? Did KIA give a glow to the sudden end of eminent activity of a loving human being? Was their death more glorious as a KIA than death from a crash of a rear echelon jeep, a non battle casualty, 'NBC'? Being accidentally killed might not have the same alleged luster as being twisted to sinew by an enemy 120 millimeter mortar round, but one was no less final than the other. What in the name of all that these dead soldiers held dear in life was enhanced by their removal as a KIA rather than a NBC?

    Shoemaker and Smith respected the enemy and his cunning. They determined the movement of tree leaves was not from an up slope breeze from the valley, but from distant weapon's lead. Our squads took cover.

    Charley's 2nd platoon was deployed to the right of the stalled squad. Charley 1st platoon to the left. They laid ripening under the sun.

    Sergeant Smith wanted no grief from enemy small arms. He crept forward to reconnoiter, then back, past his men to my section sergeant. "Put a gun on my left flank, and the other to the right, Shoe," he said. "Chinks out there have a machine gun, maybe two or three Czech brens."

    "Will do." Shoe issued the order: "1st gun to the left of Smith's squad. 2nd gun to Smith's right."

    Smith again rubbed himself with grungy earth to hide facial skin. Earth in all its forms was natural to him, a foot-soldier, who caressed its folds both day and night as shelter from the enemy and elements. Earth was a friend, whether gritted in teeth or dug by an entrenching tool. As long as an infantryman could harbor his mortal coil within earth's skirts for safety, he needed no more clothes. Smith hugged and kissed mother earth his way back to the point squad.

    Shoe watched us slip forward over rugged

terrain. Warren squeezed through heavy brush, his gun squad writhing in s-shaped curves in imitation. 2nd squad hitched and hunched on their chests like earthworms, up butt, then forward.

I did a dash with the tripod to the place Warren pointed. The tripod went quickly to ground. Clouse brought the gun forward and mounted it. He took to the prone. Bouton quickly dropped off the water can and ammo. He got back into a foxhole faster than a spring on a screen door could snap it shut.

I sat down behind the gun, upright, in a model pose with head erect observing my front as if an army photographer was there to capture me forever on film. Dirt erupted from little volcanoes beside the gun. Grit and chips leapt, some hitting my helmet like hailstones. "What?"

Warren looked back at me. There was a stunned look on his weathered face. "You're the target, Red," he screamed in astonishment. "Hit the prone."

"S-S-Shit," I exclaimed, a word learned after the seminary. I hit the prone, became a mole deep down in the soil. Sitting up behind the weapon, rear echelon perfect, cast me in the role of a volunteer for combat brevity. My hands drove the tripod's jamming handles free, the gun and cradle dropping to my low profile. I jammed tight the handles once more, then pulled the gun and tripod to new cover. I sighted, then fired a burst of six rounds to follow the tracer. I adjusted my aim for the next burst.

Sergeant Smith moved his squad past freshly dug foxholes, steadily out, considerably far in advance of the check point. The Chinese were fighting as they withdrew. Beyond their fighting spots the ridge line dipped into a shallow saddle. Smith realized if he rode the saddle without a heavy thirty, his squad would be bucked off. "Runner, get Shoe to goose a Dog heavy forward."

Shoemaker wasted no time in sending Warren's gun squad. Sergeant William Able's 2nd gun was in place to cover Smith and Warren. "2nd gun ammo bearers," called Sing. "Stack ammo. Go back to check point 16 for more."

"Yea Sarge," Ables responded. Six ammo bearers, two ROKs, Bill and John, plus Privates Norman Hart, Hubert Hansel, Arthur Sutton and Roger Stowell hurried back to Baker Company's perimeter.

Warren lined his squad behind rock outcroppings on high ground. I and Clouse hurriedly filled more of the sand bags faithfully toted up slope by the assistant gunner. "Can't you make less noise, Red," he chastised? The noise sent sharp shivers down his spine.

Smith played his binoculars on the Chinese near the saddle's horn. If it were a machine gun they were carrying to fire from the rocky point, there was going to be casualties in the 3rd squad. Yet, he knew he had to secure it. Any platoon that inched past might be rippled by flanking fire. He called the saddle horn to Warren's attention.

"Give Smith overhead support when he jumps off, Red," Warren said. "If a Chink gun opens up from the saddle horn, shift fire. Take him on, one to one. Fire," he ordered.

I let loose a heavy base of overhead support as the platoon approached the saddle, then took cover at a rock lip. The 2nd platoon jumped the embankment near by, and at five yard intervals ran just below the crest of the saddle hidden from Chinese guns opposite. All but one rifleman! His helmet flew off, and after the GI reversed directions, the blood on his forehead had the look of thick catsup.

    As if electricity coursed through Doc Davidson, our medic broke from his fox hole to reach the wounded rifleman. It was the screaming that was the worst part. Doc had to assure the terrorized GI he hadn't been captured. To little avail. Perhaps it was the exposed bone, the blood that gushed, or the pain. Doc brought the guy to his feet, nearly pushing him up the slow slope until placing him into a foxhole. Morphine was administered. Bandages put in place. Perhaps the barking laugh of the wounded man was his response to panic. Perhaps the guy thought he was a prisoner of war? Thoughts of POWs being executed by the enemy trickled like a shallow stream in the valley of every soldier's subconscious.

    I felt my heart racing a 100 yard dash. I had butterflies. I was sweating. I'd stopped firing the weapon. It wasn't killing, but being killed that turned my anxiety switch on.

    "Why aren't you firing?" Warren said.

    I didn't answer, but I did commence the beat in bursts of six. I traversed and searched the saddle horn's indentations for pests.

    Smith's squad jumped off, the other squads of the 3rd platoon echeloned to his right and left, but there was a lack of visible enemy, a worrisome omen to the high strung combat infantrymen on either side of the platoon's zone of action. Smith pushed his unit upward. He seized the crest of the horn, but where on the narrow point were the Chinese? The life pulse of combat seemed to be hushed and each rifleman looked to be a stumbling drunk. A dozen meters up, the pall of fire had shrouded the Chinese, and my shifting fire, (the safety margin rule was to not shoot up one's own buddies), had freed the enemy to pop up and fight again. Heavy small arms fire from Chink foxholes flayed the horn near its top. Aiming and firing rapidly, a GI BAR team pushed toward the redoubt. GI riflemen swept upward in a rush. There, small units struggled. The flashes of hell roared on the ridgeline. The grimaces of death dealing soldiers contorted youthful faces just off the basketball courts and football fields. Smith's squad took the horn, a geologic structure that owed its Norman tower replication to the different rates of resistance of rocks under centuries of horrible North Korean winters.

    It was the key to the next maneuver. There was no purpose in a rifle squad holding freshly dug Chinese fighting holes, giving time for the bugging enemy to regroup on the next point. Smith jumped off when Corporal Victor Torres' heavy machine gun began suppressing fire.

    Warren moved us up to the horn. Distant muzzle flashes from a Chinese machine gun was seen coming from a knob in front of the blackened outpost. The enemy's plunging rounds fell across the saddle. Warren didn't wait to be under its beaten zone. He picked a point midway to the Chinese gun, measured it by football fields and doubled the result to determine the distance. "Five hundred yards northeast," he said. "Fire."

I sent a burst of six rounds of M-2 armor piercing ammo on a projected path toward their point of impact, followed quickly by seven more bursts that searched a beaten zone on the knob. It was a duel of plunging fire, either side traversing and searching for the other's gunhole.

A strange fierce energy permeated Smith. He leaned forward from the waist, his right knee on the rocky soil, his left knee raised, every muscle tense, his head tossing his helmet forward and back. "We're jumping off, Warren. If you shift fire before you see us in those Chinks trenches, I'll run my rifle butt up your behind."

"Only find maple syrup."

Smith wanted not to smile, but he did. "Fix bayonets," he ordered.

I fired as the men of the 3rd squad lead Charley's 3rd platoon towards the crest. Shouts were heard. The squad jumped rocks taller than track hurdles, sidestepping bodies with deer footed grace. Eyes flashed lightning. Bayonets swept the crest like a steel flail, men screaming their heads off. The momentum of the attackers chased Chinamen from their fighting holes to disappear over the reverse slope. The tardy tasted icy steel. Lanced chests and backs heaved and shivered, struggling for breath. The riflemen had gone mad. They chewed up the crest blasting away, bayoneting any enemy soldier daring to tread the crimson landscape. The anger in their minds triggered round after round into every gun hole. Bedlam was a peaceful place in contrast. Smith's replacements had the spring of mountain lions, the fangs of tigers. The shadow of the stalled peace negotiations on the will to fight had passed. This new American Army, the Army of the truce talks, was turning Chinese held hills into Chinese tombs.

The slaughter dried out any need I had to relieve myself. The death shrieks lingered in my subconscious. Were the dying thirsty?

"We're supposed to be up to CP 35," Warren said. He didn't cotton to the freshly dug shallow holes, or giving time to the Chinese to fall back to the check point. He figured the enemy had a firing card on the knob and would soon let loose misery. There was concealment ahead to mount our machine guns. We could cover the 3rd platoon's advance from there. "Red, move the gun forward a hundred yards and dig in." We moved forward and dug in. Warren said to Smith, "I'll send a runner to Shoemaker to bring him and the 2nd gun up."

"How long," asked Smith?

"Does it matter if we run out of ammo on this gun? Five minutes."

Private Norb Gzregorek, grunting he'd need his old Studebaker to get back there, ran the Shoemaker detail. The section sergeant traversed the slope, the 2nd gun squad a dragon tail whirling behind. It set up. Both weapons commenced firing.

Smith pushed up out of his protective hole, jumped to his feet, and ran ahead. He yelled, "3rd squad. We're the point! Move out!"

Riflemen pushed up in sequence and followed at fifteen yard intervals, running in time. It was a cross country team, runners setting a pace calculated to get them to the finish line before their adversaries. Smith was a ridgeline soldier. He would have his squad break free from incoming by running toward the objective. He never stayed his attack long enough to get pinned down. It was his strategy, after taking an objective, to move ahead a hundred or more yards, clearing out stragglers and rear guard, removing his men from zeroed in zones. He went to the prone behind a small outcropping of stones and waited for his men to deploy. He stared down from a low puckered crest on the ridgeline into a concave draw that slowly rose to another protruding point. The whole of the scene was weird and imposing. Although it was devoid of life, there must have been a time before soldiers mounted its ridges when it palpitated with energy and beauty so high up and alone and as far removed from village life in the valley as it was. But there was no charm in this wilderness and momentary solitude. Somewhere were enemy troops. It would be a steep scramble for GI skirmishers to go up to the rocky grass grown ledge. Smith elected to flank, lest his squad should be ambushed. The day was long on into late afternoon. There were meters to go. A BAR team, its weapon with a maximum effective rate of fire per minute of 130 rounds, was set down to cover a draw. The rest of the riflemen followed. He maneuvered skirmishers toward the rock outcropping, thankful for the lull in fire from Chinese territory, appreciative for heavy thirty coverage. He constantly checked his deployment, alert to the objective, the bunching of his men, location of the units on his flanks. He advanced rapidly up the slow incline. It was a precision parade, a close order drill. He moved his squad left of the knob in a skirmish line towards the final phase of the assault. The BAR gunner took up the fire. He felt the spirit of the 3rd squad and sustained a rate of sixty rounds per minute into the bugging out enemy. He stood up in the outcropping to shoot down at the Chinese. He brought down one, then another, a third, a fourth. The BAR position went up in a furnace of flame. The gunner twisted and fell, broken apart, bloody. The shock of GIs coming up on the Chinese flank rather than their front seemed to have caught the knob's defenders by surprise. Their advantage was jeopardized. They took to running off the place like rabbits into the bush. Smith set up a firing line but they were low on ammo. He ordered, "Fix bayonets."

Several hundred yards more had to be crossed under the sights of enemy guns. There was a hundred yards between the point squad and the ridgeline's break off before the deep draw rose, leading directly into the face of dug in Chinese on the eastern half of the outpost. Smith had his men lay as close to the ground as belly buttons could wallow in the dirt. He peered across the wide divide at the bastion. It was still a long way away. Even a few hundred yards advance without massive artillery support would be on life's last thoroughfare. If there were a hell on earth, the 3rd squad had been running toward its gauntlet. Moving the 3rd platoon across the long draw would expose it to automatic fire from the saddle in the middle of the outpost.

The outpost quieted. Our machine guns fell silent.

"3rd platoon's going to attack in a 'V'," Shoe said. "3rd squad's on the left, 2nd's eighty yards to the right, taking advantage of natural coverage. Charley's light machine guns are in between the two squads and forty yards back. The other two rifle platoons are positioned either side with mortar men displacing in a defile. Fire!" Shoe's order came in concert with outgoing rounds. He wanted machine gun tracers sparkling like flashes in a charcoal fire.

The Chinese answer fire with fire, increasing its intensity. It roared to a thunderous volume. When incoming mortar rounds dropped into the draw and walked toward the platoon, Charley 3rd took to cover. No one was where they should have been. Each soldier seemed alone, abandoned.

As if they were sharp knives thrown from the brow of overhead clouds above my head, F-84s sliced through the smoke of the fire fight, blazing cannons flashing. Suddenly, plunging pieces of metal bit hunks out of my sand bags and in the earth around the fighting hole. I thought I was being hit from behind by the enemy. I grappled with Clouse to swing the machine gun around. He resisted, his eyes questioning my sanity. Then, if all the Eight Army's 155's howitzers had at that moment fired simultaneous bursts more resonate than deep thunder, my auditory senses swelled to near eruption. In confusion, I grappled Clouse to one side and took possession of the gun hole's deepest level. His knuckles bonked my helmet a few times while letting me know ear shocking sound waves always followed the planes' dives to targets. Aware at last, my heart throbbed a bit more slowly and slid out of my throat. The F-84s had turned the battle into a charnel house. Pleased with themselves for leaving a crimson glow on the far hill, they shook wings and flew away. My first glimpse of airborne's fiery oblivion hurled at Chinese infantrymen shocked me. I said a prayer for them, another of thanksgiving this infantryman wasn't over there.

Shock quickly faded when Warren made it clear the 3rd platoon was pinned down by enemy grazing fire, no GI better off than a deer in hunting season. They weren't in a quiet place. Automatic weapon fire had rippled the advancing ranks with such intensity that further advances would be through a snarling crossfire. Mortar shells fell thick to the front, their barbs hotter than branding irons. It was time for the day to die in twilight gray, a day the 1st battalion had chased Chinese for thousands of meters, but now Charley's 3rd platoon was pinned down where birds dared not whistle. They were flat on terrain where bullets zinged low. Jangled nerves had to be playing high C on the guitar strings of their synapses.

They needed help. If there were no moving up the hundred yards to the objective, how could Charley's 3rd platoon get back? I stared into the starless gloom where automatic weapon flashes freckled the dark. I was firing too high, having shifted fire to maintain the minimum clearance between the skirmishing troops and the center of the machine gun's cone of fire. The safety margin was too high. The Chinese appreciated it. "To hell with the gunner's rule!"

"You'll shoot GIs in the butt," said Clouse.

I'd followed the machine gunner's book. I'd laid the gun on the target with the correct sight setting to hit the target, then set the rear sight. Then I'd looked through the sight to note the point where his new line of aim might strike the ground. At that point I'd set the safety limit. It was the rule, but Chinese had filled the safety margin with its weaponry; and Smith had wanted close coverage.

    Clouse's eyes jerked from me to Warren, as if to suggest I get the order from the squad leader. I saw another flicker of gun flashes. I lowered my aim and fired a short blast, tracers lining the path. I adjusted, traversing and searching, turning loose a cluster of bursts. I had targets, but to make sure, crossed the enemy gun hole with the sign of a crucifix. I placed six counts where ever I saw gun flashes. I walked my tracers down slope, then across the line of enemy bunkers. I traversed and searched just above the assault area, lingering several bursts where I'd seen a communist gun flash.

    Shoemaker noted the impact the down and deep shooting was having on Chinese return fire. He yelled, "Torres! Lower fire, sight on the 1st gun's tracers."

    The 3rd section of machine guns played bursts of six across the enemy's fighting holes. Tracers bounced where the enemy was. The flashes of their weapons faded, then disappeared.

    There was a quiet out on the outpost.

"Coming in, Shoe," called Smith.

"Cease fire," Shoe ordered.

    There was a rider on Smith's right shoulder. Christie, the new BAR man, was also attired with a GI casualty. They laid the wounded down by my fighting position. Charley's Doc Doyle hurried to tend them. Chogie bearers, Korean civilians serving as litter bearers, came over. Smith said, "Christie, guard the chogies. Doc, stay with the wounded. Petruska, move the squad to positions on the firing line. I'll be there soon as I say something to Red." He looked at me. "You're a killer from a distance." He reached and shook my hand. "Your shooting got my squad out, the platoon too. Thanks!" No sooner were the words said than he left.

Warren's forehead furrowed. He said, "Smith's a soldier who isn't afraid. You've gained his and the respect of every rifleman in Charley Company. That's quite an honor, Red."

Clouse had another viewpoint, saying, "You've put our butts in a sling. Now Smith knows you run hills with a machine gun like a chogie bearer. He knows you take risks. There won't be a rifle squad in the 1st battalion that will cross an LD without you giving overhead fire. That means 1st gun out on every attack."

"No! Each rifle company has its own section of Dog thirties. The 3rd section is Charley's. We'll go when Charley goes, not Able or Baker!"

The look given me expressed sharp disagreement.

To diminish anxiety, I set about rearranging the portable ramparts. I freed a few more sand bags, filling each with gun hole soil, fitting them to place as neatly as a craftsman fitted interlocking stones. I worried what I would use for sandbags when we took the outpost. It came to me. I'd disgorge some of these bags of their fundament, and refill them up there.

My hands moved dirt while my mind worked over Smith's phraseology, 'killer from a distance'. It was less than a year ago when the fingers of my hands were folded in seminary chapel prayer. Now they pulled a trigger and turned knobs to traverse and search for communists to kill. Had I ever metamorphosed! Transformation from seminarian to soldier was done by natural agencies, changing me from the goodly to the deadly. Surely the Holy Ghost had refuge in the breasts of his Mongolian children clothed in padded cotton and Confucian philosophy. Wasn't there more than one mansion in heaven? There must be more than one road there! God, by any name, wouldn't deny His presence to any race that sought His sight unless all of China's soldiers were as atheistic as their communist leaders. I was convinced a former follower of Confucianism was as likely as a former follower of Christianity or Judaism or Islam to rediscover his beliefs in a foxhole under fire. Combat was war between believers. Back Stateside, disbelievers sat safely in the chairs of universities.

  I gave thought to my role as a killer. I wasn't a murderer. Didn't the principle of the defense of third persons free me from the appellation of murderer? Wasn't the Eighth Army a part of the United Nations effort in Korea to defend an invaded people? Didn't the Chinese rip into the U.N., defenders of the third party because the original perpetrator was about to be defeated? Wasn't killing justifiable when it was necessary as an emergency measure to avoid the imminent subjugation of the South Koreans by brutish and deadly force?

  Another version of the facts arose in my meditative process. Were the Chinese defenders of a third party against U.N. aggressors invading North Korea? I recalled doubts had been cast on the propriety of crossing the 38th parallel after the apparent defeat of the North Koreans, but were overridden by the legal theory of hot pursuit; the political theory that the 38th parallel wasn't more than a line of convenience drawn in 1945 after the end of the war with Japan solely for the purpose of accepting Japanese surrenders. Since, it wasn't a line of legal partition. It was nothing more than a line in the dirt drawn by the Soviet Union's Stalin, daring anyone to cross at their peril. Mao's troops, as General Douglas McArthur found out, were the peril.

What was the morality of combat between two defenders of third parties? Whatever theologians might have argued on that point, it was clear that the Chinese on the outpost would have decimated Charley Company if Dog machine guns hadn't become killers from a distance. Whatever the morality of freeing souls from the bodies of enemy soldiers, it wasn't by a murderer, it was by a soldier loyal to his outfit.

I broadened the application of Smith's phrase to mortar men, artillerymen, even quad-fifties and tankers, all killers from a distance; albeit, the distance from the enemy varied greatly to the proximity of the hot barrel of the heavy machine gun, M1917 A1, to the enemy. Would the concept of justifiability apply to the governments in Washington, Peking and Moscow? Not with the same implications as applied to soldiers.

Were all politicians in these governments murderers? They were in Moscow when they knowingly planned the military invasion of South Korea for its forcible subjugation, or even for any other purpose that took the lives of the innocent. Murder was a willful, knowing, deliberate, premeditated act that killed or caused the killing of another human being.

Did the artificial division of Korea provide a legal basis for the north to invade? There was no substance to that argument. Korea stayed divided only because Stalin wanted it so. Stalin had no persuasive influence in the south. He would have had if the Imum Gun (North Korean Army) had taken Pusan before the Americans came! So the Soviets and North Koreans were murderers, but not the United States and the United Nations, if the attack of the Eighth Army across the 38th parallel was legally justified. Did it happen only because General MacArthur, an extraordinarily competent field general deliberately removed from action the X corps, his anvil, before the pursuing Eighth Army, his hammer, could destroy the fleeing North Koreans, letting them escape? What if General MacArthur did this for a pretext to cross the 38th, conquer the north, and sit on a Manchurian pony? These were mad thoughts; fluttering wildly, tumbling about a mind that sought explanations that didn't come easily.

I ducked into my gun hole at the blast of a Chinese grenade down the perimeter. It wasn't far away. An enemy wanted my gun to fire, a trick to discover the exact location of automatic weaponry. I marveled at the guts of infantrymen, Chinese and GI, who probed fighting positions by flipping grenades at suspects. They hoped a jumpy trigger finger might reveal its location to a forward observer. A hell of an occupation, prober that was, not observer. I felt no honor that the probe was for my machine gun. Instinct kept my head behind cover as the blasts of two more heavy concussion grenades rippled the air and propelled rocks off stone. It sounded like cracking whips. Another three explosions followed, coming closer each time. Somewhere on this somber mountain, I hoped at least one GI was glancing down from his gun hole. I knew I wasn't the one. I worried no one on the perimeter wanted to fire and reveal themselves.

"Coming in," Warren said, sliding into my deepened fighting position. "Just a probe looking for you, Red. Keep your head down. Use carbines or they'll drop a load. We're waiting for the right moment. Don't shoot unless some Chink rips up here to bayonet you." He saw a nest of owl eyes. "Sergeant Smith has a system."

I worried that Smith's system meant the machine gun crew was the bait in which the fish hook bayonets of the Chinese would lodge. I pulled my head close to the sand bags for cover at the sounds of the unexpected eruptions and zings of GI fragmentation grenades about ten yards down, and across the perimeter line. When I saw white phosphorus grenades light the black desolation either end of the fragmentation explosions, I looked over the sand bags and saw Chinese bugging into a torrent of luminous wax and gun fire, and one at a time, from front to the fourth man, were hit.

"That's Smith's system," said a delighted Warren.

Came a quiet after his departure and my cogitative processes returned to philosophical reflections. I reasoned that whatever the motives of General MacArthur, the law allowed pursuit of fleeing felons, their accomplices no less guilty than the perpetrators. I held the Chinese were the murderers, having intervened with deadly force against an army justified to defend friends. Additionally, so were North Korean's leaders because of atrocities inflicted by its soldiers on bound and gagged captured GIs. China had plotted its murderous adventure. It had no right of sanctuary as against the rights of every dead South Korean and executed American soldier.

I reasoned on another theory, conspiracy. The Chinese government knew the Soviets were reequipping and relocating North Korean infantry and tank divisions in the Iron Triangle area, for China's army also reequipped and relocated divisions on North Korea's border. They did this with the purpose of promoting the original invasion. They did it in concert. When the North Koreans were finally put to flight the final act of the conspiracy was played in November 1951! Indeed the Chinese were murderers!

I questioned if stateside politicians were killers from a distance; or murderers. President Harry S. Truman had authority over MacArthur. The President and his Joint Chiefs of Staff might have kept the X corps southwest of the 38th parallel as the anvil while the Eighth Army hammered the core of the North Koreans. There would have been no threat left to chase north. Neither the President nor his Joint Chiefs did. While the decision was political, the Commander in Chief and his Joint Chiefs of Staff left the decision of crossing the 38 parallel to a majestic General flushed with the success of Inchon.

Clouse stirred. He needed to do more than peer from the gun hole across the saddle. He spoke of the day's heavy resistance compared with that just three months ago, worried if there were any bit of Korea ahead that would give him less of the awestruck shudders than those he had undergone on this attack. What had happened to joy with the coming of the truce talks, those dreamy wishes of home by Labor Day? Was the regiment launched upon a war of attrition?

The grim face of the outpost looked to me more primevally savage in the darkness than in sunshine, particularly when the thunder of distant howitzers announced dancers going to rehearsal on the outpost's dark haunts. The overhanging crest of the objective looked as if it might at any moment topple down from the pounding. I saw rocks over there as big as oblong hay stacks on every acre, a place that was one vast chaotic upheaval of inorganic and organic matter wrought into fearful shapes. Above, clouds appeared to be contriving to organize dissidents, as if bidding them to avoid the glaring searchlights of field illumination; to no avail.

I felt the wind's breath, and wondered how a man from the Midwest became a slave to these high haunts? It was my lot to work hard, to be infantry. But why, in this month and year of Our Lord, September 1951, had mechanization of the water cooled heavy machine gun apparently ended its progress in 1917, the year it was first used against the Kaiser's soldiers. Wouldn't America go into debt to buy modern machinery? Was that it with the United States Army and its M1917 A1? On the other hand, one didn't need to be the best equipped if equipment at hand was sufficient. It strained imagination to conjure a heavy weapon better suited to fight roaring battles with massed men on the attack, particularly in the hands of a killer from a distance, bred to sing the machine gun's anthem in battle in harmony with the dread engines of war of the destructive 35th Regiment, 25th Division.

Dawn was walking in. My eyes returned to the misshapen peaks on the outpost. Warren hustled over. "Snap to it. Our section of heavy thirties covers Able Company's riflemen!"

They moved out stoically. What else could they do but keep nose to neck so as not to go north all alone. Predawn marching on an unfamiliar topography wasn't much to an infantryman's liking where there wasn't even a rugged path. In one's mind he could see the face of the outpost, but eyes saw but a few feet to the front, combat boots grappled with rocks, olfactory senses inhaled wisps of sulphur the yards stumbled before a halt and restart. White phosphorus, 'WP', came in to mark caves in which Chinese might escape from bombardment but not from a fluid inferno that peeled eyelids like potato chips.

As if WP were a burst from a brilliant sun releasing billows of smoke as white as dove wings enfolding a beauteous red rose, it marked the target for circling Corsairs that banked away to form a line of flight to hit the designated vapors. As the yellowish red phosphorus shone through the smoke of the crimson fringed outpost, Chinese mortar men retaliated. A round of their own white phosphorus fell between the line of departure and the attacking Able platoon. A Corsair was decoyed to redirect its fire. Under its drop, the field between the attacking GI platoon and Dog's 1st section of machine guns writhed and withered. I watched horrified as the fluid spread its searing liquid and billowing flames. A sergeant pumped his arm up and down rapidly. He would get his troops to the rock stump line as quickly as he could, preferring his chances against small arms and automatic weapons than against a friendly crematory.

"Fire mission," Shoe called. "Right front! Across the lower trench line. 1st gun, take the right half. 2nd gun, fire the left half. Two hundred! Traverse! Rapid fire! At my command." He paused to check readiness. "Fire!"

We watched our tracers hone home, then moved two mills between bursts to distribute the bullets impacting each target. Riflemen made good use of terrain. Their eyes honed in on the tracer line as if it were a highway center line guiding them to their objective. They moved forward with as relentless a perseverance as the drumming heavy thirties. Able Company seemed to seethe with a peculiarly aggressive morale. Its infantrymen bristled as they attacked, bayonets fixed to close with killing strokes; the long point and the short point of sharpened steel. From a spur came automatic weapon fire ranging in, the lead squad of skirmishers taking casualties. They came to a temporary halt. Our guns' eruption of answering tracers gave range to friendly mortars and suppressing counter fire. The weapon on the spur fell silent. The assault squad arose in near unison from opposite flanks, and ran straight for the spur. GIs' death curses sprang with a vengeance to not leave an enemy alive. Casualties taken on the charge didn't discourage the unscathed soldiers from weaving in and out of loose stone and rock outcroppings with quick steps. Hard breathing GIs plunged into the vacated holes screaming at the withdrawing enemy, firing at bugouts, killing any slow to surrender. Working nearer Chinese trenches, rifleman crouched over broken ground, through craters, over ditches, toward the trench line connecting caves and bunkers, firing at targets of opportunity, tossing in grenades. Gunfire splattered across the spur. GIs closed with a roar. An exhausted GI laid down among the deceased on the ghastly rock. It was a dreadful struggle, the enemy fleeing in bloody disarray. Within this mad and awful tumult, I watched helmets and cotton caps churn. Then I shifted fire into the bugging enemy.

    An eerie quiet fell over the darkly shadowed trenches and winds whispered from the caves on the outpost of the dead. A mortal calm had fallen. Bleeding bodies beneath the grim dust of the battle shaded gristly remains from the morning sun. There were torn Chinese in deadly poses, severed forever from their five senses; bone and sinew divided. On the somber mountain of spectral trenches, blackened bodies crowded the trench line, sprawled in hideous lumps. Intestines oozed. Bloody shreds of flesh appeared to have been ripped from cadavers by rapacious lions. Torn skin puckered in volcanoes with innards poised as if lava were ready to pour forth. Mouths gaped widely. Lifeless eyes stared at palls of dark flies stuck to drying blood. While there might have been hope before the truce talks failure for an end to such unseemly slaughter, I foresaw battle banners flying in a fiercely flaming sky.

    The battle for the outpost was a test of human life blood during the havoc of sleeping truce talks. It was a new war, a rock to rock, ridgeline to crest warfare. It was combat on the hill tops, a new era of siege surge!

If not the Eighth Army, the 25th Division's 35th Regiment was a deluge of destruction!

SOLE SURVIVING SON

I had come of age in a land of bloodshed among soldiers marshaled for the deadly toil of war. The 25th Division's 35th Regiment's combat action on the Outpost pronounced me a combat infantryman, a man among fighting men nearly six months before my twenty first birth day. I'd be eligible at age 21 to vote for or against my Commander in Chief, Harry S. Truman, the President of the United States.

No day in the Army was as thrilling as that day, September 10, 1951, not because my outfit, the 1st Battalion, retook the Outpost on hill 682 in the morning; but because in the afternoon we were pulled off the front to return to the rear. Reserve again! It meant we backed up the outfits on the front line, but it also meant ongoing training. Blocking position was also off the front line, but much closer with prepared fighting positions in case the enemy broke through the front. Odds of survival were far higher in reserve than on the Outpost or on the Main Line of Resistance. The MLR was up north a mile or so and a mountain or two between the valley we were to occupy. The whole of Korea, north or south was mountainous, each mountain with fingers, ridges that ran down from the high points to a valley. Many of the hills retained trees, but most had been splintered to toothpicks. Weeds and grasses were green, that was, where not blacked by napalm or explosions.

Every bone in my body ached, but every step coming down the hill put me in a convivial mood. My tour of the outpost's environs had lasted three days as the calendar recorded it, but by the calculations of stress, three years. Each step southward was far more relaxing than those northward. In the south was hot food, hot showers and warm cots. Behind, was the debris of death.

It would be quite a switch, from dirt holes to tent flaps, from whistling shrapnel to barbershop quartets, from cheese and bacon rations to slabs of hot tender beef. Hot coffee would be as potent a trance producer as cold milk. Sleep would follow! I wouldn't be late for supper or somnolence. I thought no more of the mortuary on the mount!

Shoemaker and Warren were talking of nothing else. They were bewildered at the order for the entire 35th Regiment to pull off the outpost with Baker Company to hold hill 432. A bit late. Warren said he understood why the full regimental attack was launched to break through to the trapped 3rd battalion, but not why the 35th was now abandoning the outpost in favor of hill 432. He knew he wasn't a military genius, but whatever the military tactic in giving up the outpost was, it wasn't clear. It left the Chinese with hills 1062, 717, 682 and 598, the high ground!

Shoe felt the 25th Infantry Division had gone as far north in Kumhwa as the Eighth Army and the United Nations Forces would ever go. The blue gloom of the burned hills marked the boundaries of the future. The 1st battalion had fought only because a sister battalion had been cut off, not because of a general order to attack. Proof was in this withdrawal. Clearly the regiment had been ordered to pull back, stand and hold. The line had been drawn! A signal to the Chinese that the 25th Infantry's present battle line at Kumhwa was it, no more, no less!

So there it was, as Shoe continued to spout off, the tactics of the US government and the Far East Command: to hold what we had. His remaining time in Korea would be in trenches, a reversionary tactic to the First World War. Wasn't that President Truman's war? The reality of an obviously conceded battle line set by ghostly politicians was apparent. The machine gun section would pull its future in conflict deep within trenches.

Shoe's breathing changed. He halted our march down hill. Short intense breaths wheezed like an old dog's panting through a deviated septum. He looped back, passed Warren, and stopped at me. He opened my back pack, freed a beer, cut a smile in the lid, raised the can in a toast and said, "Here's to meaningless objectives like the outpost, GIs lost, my faith in Eight Army's War Tent."

We worked down the fingers, back up hills and down again until there was a valley and base camp. Flat areas down slope were called valleys, but level ground there was even at a premium. Rest assured, however, the Company Command Post, CP, and officers' tents hugged the flat places.

Hot chow! I savored the beef. It was putting roses back on my grimy cheeks and a glint in each eye that before had stared hundreds of yards at targets. The barrel bottom chef's culinary skills did more than equal justice to each pound of meat I inhaled to diminish gustatory grumbling. Usually, skilled cooks were kept for officers' mess, the best back in battalion, regiment and division. Line company's got Army trained cooks, not professionals.

Nonetheless, I was in infantry heaven. There was a hill between me and the front line. There were tents with cots awaiting the section of machine guns, not pup tents and a sleeping bag on hard ground. A hot shower waited down by the river, clean clothes with the supply sergeant. I looked forward to clothes not plastered to skin by sweat, grit and dirt. For the moment though, my mess kit bulged with the bounty from a hot field stove; canteen cup oozed with cold milk. I was alive, eating, drinking and grinning as inanely as Private Baldy Heideman. His lack of scalp hair, a perpetual grin, wide eyes with a dazed gaze, might have classed him with cretins. Others of my squad wore Baldy's lunatic look. They were alive, eating and drinking, a colony of grinning baboons chowing down on fermented figs!

"HQ thinks line troops will eat rat with body heat restored," Warren said. "They figure combat soldiers think c-rations are steak after a diet of combat rations; hot food a delicacy no matter the skill of the cook. Why waste good cooks on cast iron guts? Only reason we got the fatted calf as cook was back in stateside messes he only showed skill in cutting heifers' carcasses into serviceable cuts. Didn't flash a hint he had minimal cookery inclinations. When he put his belly near a stove, they worried he'd flavor the soup with sweat dripping from his overhanging porch. Mess officers shipped him out, Dog the end of the line. Ever since his first cooked meal, we put a muzzle on so the word doesn't get back to S-1."

"Fat chance," Diemer said, spewing food. He was the other GI in our squad to rival the demented look of Heideman. "Be no rear echelon crud who volunteer to visit a line company. Cook safe!"

    I looked with admiration at the becircled being encapsulated as if by a turf clump, who could burp loud as a tuba. He had no fear of the powers in the rear echelon. Where could they ship him worse than where he was? How could they ever check up on him if they did? The rear echelon transcribed combat reports. They didn't dictate them. I didn't mind the burp of appreciation for deliciously prepared hot food, I did the decided olfactory dissatisfaction for the subsequent punctuation out his other end!

    The day's training over, and back in the squad tent, I hit the prone and heard this:

    "Sergeant Shoe, when you think I visit mon frere? Top Kick doing nothing." Private Jacques Boudreau was the inquirer. "I hear 9th Regiment on Bloody Ridge! My brother, Pierre, up there."

    "Tell you what, Boudreau," Shoe said, "Red's on his butt back there. He's college stuff, educated up his nose. Probably knows the Chaplain. How about you and Red figure it out?"

    Boudreau had bothered the section sergeant once too often. I measured the assignment as one calculated to keep the Cajun from more interference with Shoe's parties and poker games. The bushel chest Sergeant First Class kept his cot in the 1st gun's squad tent where Bill ROK, a stub of a Korean soldier assigned to the US Army, could tend to the needs of the players. Bill ROK used ammo box wood to fabricate Shoe's poker table and chairs, a dresser with drawers of metal ammo boxes, a chest of boxes reminiscent of hardware bins, and a peg board to hang field gear. I didn't have to guess why the cots were closely clustered in opposite rows either side of the tent toward its rear, with a double lantern on the front tent pole near the poker table. Shoe had made over the inside of the tent into a Las Vegas store house of rustic military antiques.

Boudreau, disgusted with the sergeant, nodded okay.

I, too, nodded okay. Boudreau came over. I'd met the Catholic Chaplain at Mass before the attack against the outpost. He looked Irish. After Mass, I introduced myself by pronouncing 'Father' as 'feather' as my father's brogue spoke it, and said: "Maybe our families met before. You see, Father, our ancestors in Ireland over seven hundred years ago met when the Irish kicked the tails of the invading Walshs."

The cleric's wind whipped reddened face expressed considerably more than quizzical interest. A removed cassock revealed a gaunt and muscular frame, fatigues streaked with sweat; eyes questionable. "And you're a Walsh."

"Private Red Walsh, Dog machine guns." We talked a while, his interest acute when I told him I'd left the Seminary in my third year of college to join the Army. He too, had volunteered, though his Bishop wasn't keen on it. Our conversation led to a suggestion I look into being a chaplain's assistant. I thanked him, but having enlisted to fight a war, I didn't want to watch it from the Altar.

"Coup de main. Helping hand," said Boudreau, looking down at me. "On the bayou, families and friends help each other." He let loose a Charles De Galle smile. Boudreau was tall and bony, features sharp, face cadaverous. "Pierre and me, we in Korea. Le Bon Dieu will help me visit Pierre."

    I rolled my feet off the cot to the ground and sat up. "When we go to Mass next, we can ask His priest." A 2x2 truck drove all who wanted to attend religious services back to Battalion HQ. After the battle for the outpost, the beauty in the prayers of the Mass were never more joyful. My mind floated back to St. Mary's Seminary in Mundelein, Illinois, to Sacred Heart Seminary in Detroit, to the days when I read Chaucer in the study hall; studied Latin and Greek; beat off the Sophomore class raid of the Freshmen's dorm; had visitors on Sundays before vespers; played baseball on its green clad diamond; basketball in the gym; handball in the four wall courts. I relished the shade of the tree-lined campus' circular walkway; the lectures in the class rooms; the magnificence of the choir at solemn high Mass. I hadn't known it was such a banquet of glory, but I hadn't known combat. How bright ran my memories of the seminary now, seeing as I was several thousand miles away. Mass over, Boudreau on my tail, we hurried to tie up the Chaplain before others cornered him after services. "Feather," I said, "A moment please." I had his attention, but our truck was reloading for the return trip. I came to the point. "Father, this is PFC Jacques Boudreau. He is also in Dog Company, the 35th. He has a brother, PFC Pierre Boudreau, Easy Company, 9th Regiment, 2nd Division. Will you help them visit?"

    "I'll work on it," the Chaplain answered, while writing in a notebook, "but the 9th has been in battle since a ROK regiment was driven off hill 983 by the North Koreans." His eyes told us there was a story there. He told it. "The North Koreans tunneled the entire ridgeline. It's a nearly vertical hill with concentrated fields of fire. Every time the 9th attacks the razor sharp ridgeline, they walk the backbone of a raging bear. The enemy pops out from camouflaged bunkers nestled like beaver mounds over grass." The truck revved its motor. "Better catch your rides, Jacques, Red. Come to Mass next week. I should have something."

Boudreau left to mount the truck. My arm was grabbed from behind before I could leave to do so.

"Just a minute, Red," said the Chaplain. "I'll tell you, but I couldn't tell Jacques. Casualties are high up there. 2,700 among the ROKs and the 9th Infantry; 15,000 for the North Koreans. It's a blood bath, meat-grinder combat with elements of both the ROKs and the 9th Infantry being fed piecemeal. Regiment finally woke and committed all its battalions at once. Perhaps Pierre's okay."

"I hope so," I said. "Pierre is his only brother."

Back to Dog Company, didn't Reserve end. The 1st Battalion was ordered up. We relieved the 27th Regiment on the MLR. I couldn't believe that outfit had barely dug in. The bunker assigned for my machine gun was no deeper than a few feet with scattered branches for a roof and few sand bags. Clouse, Bouton and I labored digging in, lugging tree trunks up slope, filling sand bags enough to diminish the Sahara desert several feet. Coming off the MLR for Mass was special. Death was always with an infantryman. During services, I reflected on the language of Boudreau's prayers during Mass. Were they in French, Cajun or English?

"Hoc est enim Corpus Meum, For this is My Body," said the priest. The mystery of Transubstantiation celebrated, communion distributed, the Mass ended.

I was impressed with the piety and devotion displayed by line troops. Communion put God there too. Many were the prayers to see them safely through until the happy day of a cease fire. Many were the prayers to God to motivate atheistic politicians, their side and ours, to meet and talk and end this police action.

I recognized Father's frequent sighs were more than a visit warranted. There was no other purpose for this meeting than to complete visitation arrangements for the brothers. This day was just right for it. Light rains had ceased, the temperature was in the very comfortable sixties and low rolling clouds were a blanket over the troubles of the MLR. Yet emotionalism in the cleric was impatient of restraint. "Red, Jacques," he said as if intoning 'Dies irae,' "come, sit in my jeep." We followed him and Jacques took the front seat. Father stood facing Jacques. "I've written countless letters home for GI's to their loved ones, many about soldiers killed in action. I've talked to squads, platoons, even companies, expressing the grief they couldn't permit themselves when a buddy fell." He paused. "I wept for them and now I weep with you, Jacques. Pfc. Pierre Boudreau of the 2nd Division, 9th Regiment was killed in action on September 15 on hill 894."

Boudreau leaned forward on the Padre's jeep hood. He appeared to be looking to me. Was it for an explanation? I hadn't one. I'd hoped to conclude a visitation plan. After the outpost, I now had some idea of the hideous nervous strain which had fallen on one soldier who had lost not just a buddy, but a brother to combat. Boudreau deserved to be set free of it.

 Father was unwontedly emotional, tears in his eyes. "When the 23rd regiment hadn't taken hills 931 and 851, the 9th was sent against hill 728 on September 14 to relieve the pressure. They had fire support from the 72nd tanks, but the North Koreans were sending over long range fire. Still, at 0200 hours the 9th attacked within 600 or so meters of the crest before they formed a night perimeter. Next day, after hours of hard fighting, the 9th's second battalion took 894, despite heavy machine gun fire. Your brother was hit. I was told he, before he passed on, pulled some wounded from an open area raked by enemy fire." Father sat down on the Jeep's hood mournful as the mournful brother. "Your brother's regiment had the support of the First French Battalion. It was their chaplain that informed me 'Pierre Boudreau vient d'etre tue. Pierre Boudreau was just killed.' Father's voice was soft, modulated with empathy. "Pierre will be returned home to be buried."

 I watched the last son of the Boudreau's walk slowly away from the consoling priest as if the Cajun had had enough sympathy. He should feel better knowing his brother would be ferried stateside to be buried near the water and banks that he had known as a boy, not overseas in Korea, but in the bayous with his ancestors, a long litany of Cajun Americans.

 As if a stage master gave a cue, the reflection on Boudreau's ancestry told me that Jacques was the last of the Boudreau line. His brother hadn't lived to father a child. Nor had he! There were no other brother for the Army to expend. If the Army were to have a future opportunity to recruit Boudreaus to its ranks, then the bow and arrow of the Kumhwa soldier should be broken in favor of cupid's. He was a sole surviving son, momentarily. I was determined to reenlist the commiserating priest's efforts toward Boudreau's reassignment out of a combat unit. "Jacques is a sole surviving son, Father, get him home!"

"Is that right? I'll get my friend from the Red Cross to check it out," the tear stained priest said, now smiling.

"Get him off the line now, Father," I said, pressing.

"It's not within my power."

"You said you needed a Chaplain's Assistant," I said. My deuce-by was revving its coughing motor.

"I'll get on it." Father gave me Our Lord's salutation.

I saluted the religious officer, recognizing an oxymoron. The American Red Cross managed Boudreau's transfer Stateside.

CREW DRILL

Sergeant First Class George Shoemaker, leader of Dog Company's third section of heavy machine guns, snapped to his squad leaders, "Warren, Ables, ready your gun crews for drill."

They ordered the three man gun crews to intervals of five yards apart, the gunner first, the others in a straight line behind the gunner. I, the 1st squad's gunner, had at my side a fifty-one pound tripod with legs folded; Private Hartland Clouse, assistant gunner, a forty-three pound machine gun and Private William Bouton, first ammo-bearer, a water-can and a 250 round can of ammo weighing twenty pounds. For the 2nd gun squad, Corporal Victor Torres was gunner, Private Francis Painter, assistant gunner and Private Norman Hart, 1st ammo bearer.

Action," the squad leaders yelled in unison while pointing to positions where they wanted their guns mounted.

I sprung to my feet as if jumping from a rattlesnake. I grasped the mount, swung it to my right hip and dashed to the point like a shot arrow, my tripod's frontal legs flying out. Torres was close behind, his tripod's legs swinging like broken tree limbs. Clouse high stepped behind me and aligned the gun over the cradle as I rammed tight the tripod legs' jamming handles. Painter hadn't a cradle in which to place his gun until he helped Torres jam the legs' handles and pull out the locking pin from the cradle. The gun was finally seated. Bouton had our water can next to our mounted weapon, water hose attached and was opening the ammo-can when I raised the rear sight of the gun. Clouse inserted the tab of the ammo-belt into the weapon. I pulled the ammo-belt tab to the right, cocked the gun to half load and shouted "up!"

"Ready," answered Clouse.

"Out of action," Warren ordered.

I pulled the gun's cover to the rear with my left hand and then raised it with the right. Clouse removed the belt of ammo from the feedway. He replaced the belt in the ammo-can, closing it; removed the hose and inserted the water plug into the gun. Bouton, Clouse and I, as if one, resumed the prone back where we'd started, rearranging the equipment with military orderliness. Torres, Painter and Hart were still forward.

"Warren," Torres grunted on his way back, "do it again for a week's ration of beer?" He flashed a snake's smile. "Hey Red?"

It wasn't going dry for a week that bothered me. It was winning, for Torres had a permanent seat at Shoemaker's poker table. A wrong word dropped to the section Sergeant would subject me to every detail to which a Private soldier was heir. I conjured up an honorable out. "There's two others to ask. How about it Clouse? Bouton? You must be burned out."

"Hey," Torres said, his smile a quarter moon, "each crew puts up the week's beer."

Bouton took him on. "Let's run 2nd gun off the hill." With Clouse nodding agreement what could I do? I had a deal with both Clouse and Bouton, my issued cigarettes for their beer. If we lost, would they insist I still owed them the cigarettes? No beer to me? I worried more about the beer than work details. We took our position, equipment beside us. Every tissue in my body ready to go. Torres' crew was restless. His pride was at stake, not the beer. Warren , Ables and Shoemaker stood ten yards ahead and gave the order. "Action."

I had a yard on Torres as I jammed the jamming handles tight and sat down. Clouse slipped the gun into the cradle like an ink pen into an ink well. Bouton churned earth, spilling not a drop from the water can to wet the dust down. Ammo was fed the machine gun. "Up," I called.

"Out of action," ordered Warren.

Bouton returned for his water can and ammo. Clouse had the gun on his hip like a mother her baby. I replaced the front locking pin, leapt up and swung the tripod over my right hip heading for the starting position. "Up," I shouted. Victory!

3.2 percent beer might have been barely fermented, but it never tasted so good.

INCOMING

Surprising as it might seem to civilians, there were times in Korea when a front line soldier appreciated silence from shelling by our artillery on the enemy. This night in Kumhwa our outgoing artillery had neutralized the enemy's return incoming fire. Anxiety faded as fast as our rounds exploded. No sane Chink infantry would dare probe our positions. Hopefully, as darkness was slipping up the hill, our artillery wouldn't let up.

The trench was coming along. Two diggers, Private Sergio LaSapio and I dug for safety and survival while Private Laverne 'Baldy' Heideman sat in a near-by shell hole spooning brown goo out of a c-ration can into his cavernous mouth. A flare popped above and floated down, its throb lighting our dig. Baldy's tonsure seemed a reflecting mirror. LaSapio and I hit the bottom of the trench, Baldy came in on top of us, covering like a blanket. Another flare popped and floated like a butterfly. Anxiety returned. I slowly untangled and raised my head and M2 Carbine to a firing position, praying no stray bullet was timed to hit below my helmet's lip. No enemy in sight!

Back in 1st squad's machine gun bunker, assistant gunner Private Hartland Clouse said, "Red, me and Truscott got time on you, but you're on the weapon, take what guard you want."

I took the first two hours, followed by Truscott, then Clouse. They sat down on a poncho in the gunhole. Clouse started wrapping a shelter half around himself but was asleep before it was done. Private Carroll Truscott, 1st Ammo Bearer, joined

Clouse on the poncho, but pulled the shelter half over himself. I peered into space and saw its vastness, a void. Where was my nearest supporting foxhole? I saw the second squad's machine gun position to my left. Was it thirty miles away? My squad leader, Staff Sergeant Dean Warren was dug in to the right. Yet I felt fascinated. I was on the front line of a major battlefield, rosy tongues of flame sprouting above the enemy's positions before our big guns went to bed.

    A distant moaning sigh suddenly changed to a horrible roar. The earth around my gunhole was in motion. The slope of my field of fire writhed. Another terrible convulsion. Horrendous noises followed. One explosion furiously hurled stones high. I smelled the stench of cordite. The ground near me was erupting as if it were in the mouth of a volcano. Everything was hissing and sizzling, shrapnel falling like a hot shower. Chunks of the mountain flew everywhere. How was I to fight back? I dared not raise my head above the lip of the machine gun aperture. Prayer came. "Lord have mercy on my soul!"

    Clouse and Truscott were awake, eyeing me. They'd better, otherwise, thoughts of bugging out might have risen with the smoke of powder. Bug out where? Incoming was hitting everywhere. A glare flashed. There was an up welling plume like a spotlighted water spout. They coiled like snakes in a pit. I sat down low and covered my head and helmet with arms I hoped were steel. How could we fight incoming rounds? Would the next one drop on our bunker? Could it withstand the explosion? Would we be consumed, vaporized? Graves Registration might not have enough of any of us to know which was which. A shell blazed grit. A cone of dirt buzzed. The earth shook, rumbling like a giant clearing his throat. Clouse nor Truscott unwrapped. I tugged my helmet below my pug nose to my clenched teeth. "Lord have mercy on our souls." I rolled my tongue, gurgled, choked. My nerves felt like shredded wheat.

    As suddenly as the crashes of every caliber of incoming fire came, the enemy as suddenly shifted fire, walking the incoming dog eastwardly down the trench line like a succession of waves on a beach. Then silence! It was as terrifying as were incomings' tremendous shocks. I rose, taking a firing position to peer down the slope into the abyss of the valley. Nothing up close. Darkness had stolen the far hills. We checked chests, legs, every external bodily part. We were whole but ears' drums pounded.

    With the rise of the sun, I got a good look at the enemy's handiwork. I shivered. That crater to our front hadn't been there before. It was enormous. The hill's nob was gone. The whole perimeter was cratered as if we were on the moon!

I REMEMBER OPERATION CACTI

The morning of 25 October 1951, 3rd section of Dog Company's heavy .30 caliber machine-guns assigned to support Charley Company was pulled from the Main Line of Resistance, MLR. We walked reverse slope's rocky trail to Baker Company to attack with Able Company when good sense asked why. Rumor had it the truce talks turned back on.

Sergeant First Class George Shoemaker, a tough Ohioan, pushed us. Stride after stride below hills' brows our two squads and Corporal Wilbur "Doc" Davidson, our Missouri medic, stomped dirt. We passed through melting mists. Our breathing labored on Line Wyoming's mountains which never seemed to descend. A chill wind crept by, tickling the mist into mystical forms and feathery whirls. A faint eastern gleam pierced the misty blueness behind us.

Ables' riflemen clustered below Baker's Command Post, CP, around a reverse slope garbage sump. My squad leader, Staff Sergeant Dean Warren, an Iowan, saw the garbage pit in perspective, given the circumstances of lead soon to be flying. We hopped in at his order and parked atop the waste. 2nd gun's gunner, Corporal Victor Torres, a Californian, was more elegant. He sat on the edge dangling legs. We crunched down as far as malleable flesh would allow. Down slope were shot-up tree branches that looked witches fingers hung with hazy ornaments. Stars were fading into a vastness of gold. Up slope were the bowled legs of riflemen, a consequence of lugging rifles, grenades, bandoleers of ammo, entrenching tool, canteen, first-aid packet and in back packs, combat-rations, hopefully not cheese and bacon. My pack carried socks, combat rations, three well-oiled spare parts for the weapon, each wrapped in a GI olive drab washcloth to not dent my half dozen 3.2 beer cans. A termite grenade was looped on a pack suspender. If in danger of being overrun by the enemy, I was instructed to use the grenade to melt the machine-gun that it not fall into their hands. Nothing was said about whose hands this gunner shouldn't fall into. Ripping the air to enemy territory was a raging torrent of artillery shells with proximity fuses exploding above their fighting holes. Once our artillery and mortars lifted fire, we'd jump off into counter fire. Jump off was but a tick away, and time was double timing to it.

    Dog Six, Company Commander, his expression dismayed over the squatting on trash, gave the word. From 1st section's bunkers to the right and 2nd section's to the left of the Line of Departure, LD, four machine-guns would lay down covering fire when Able's 3rd platoon jumped off at 0835 hours. Shoemaker's section would follow in file and dig in when the first check point was seized. Our weapons providing overhead fire, an Able squad would take the next check point. Able 3 and our 3rd section were to take the final objective. Dog Six said in conclusion, "I'd wished I could go on this attack, but I'll be watching through my binoculars." The words lacked inspiration.

    In my humble opinion, 1st section deserved the honor of attacking with Able. I wouldn't have hesitated to take over their fortified bunkers and fire from cover! The ground shook! Shrapnel sung. The eruption's fallout pounded my helmet, my head inching up within. I saw a column of earth and smoke. Who was hit? Two riflemen. Medics tended them. But for the garbage sump, never mind the jibe about 'maggots in a bung hole', 3rd section's men might have been counted among the casualties.

"Saddle up," Shoemaker barked. I mounted the machine-gun's 51 pound tripod on my shoulders, two legs forward, held by my arms like a cross. At that moment, I'd never forgotten to pray. Assistant gunner Private Hartland Clouse, now beyond the reach of two women's Pennsylvania subpoenas, carried the 41 pound machine-gun. First ammo bearer Private William Bouton, a quiet type, carried a water can and a can of ammo. Warren carried my M-1 carbine on his left shoulder, his M-1 rifle, a cleaning rod down its bore, on his right, a set of spare parts in his pack. An extra barrel was neatly wrapped and attached to his pack. Up at the LD came the order to 'move out'. To do it, for every soldier knew he was moving into enemy fire, took unfathomable courage.

Able's platoon leader deployed his skirmishers. Shoemaker ordered us to the right flank. Every inch forward was a climb. The first check point looked a rotted molar on a long, gummy ridgeline. It was taking considerable artillery. 60 and 81 millimeter tubes belched rounds to destroy land mines that might blow off feet, barbed wire that might slow the advance. 250 yards out, enemy burp guns spat like babies. Grenades, erupting with resonant booms and thick as mosquitoes in a swamp, flew toward our skirmishers.

"Action," ordered Shoemaker. Warren directed my weapon to a position behind a stone ten yards forward. 2nd gun squad leader William Ables had

Torres set up to the left. Spread in an arc to fight were Ammo bearers Privates Carroll Truscott from Utah; Laverne Heideman, bald as a rock; Joseph Geiger, transferred from the 24th Regiment after the Army finally integrated its fighting men; Sergio LaSapio, New York; Thomas Diemer, California, our most bedraggled troop; Norman Hart, Virginia; Francis Painter, Texas; Hubert Hansel, Ohio; Arthur Sutton, Wisconsin; Roger Stowell, Minnesota; Norbert Gzregorek, Indiana; new recruit Leonard Griscones, Pennsylvania, and Im Ta Song, alias Joe ROK, a Republic of Korea soldier.

  I fired across the top of a stone wall. Tracers did a dance, yet the long traverse of arcing grenades continued. The attack of riflemen slowed. To the right, down a sharp incline, the corner of my eye caught movement. I ceased firing and slapped free the tripod's cradle pintle clamp to swing the gun right. I pushed Clouse forward of the gun tripod and clamped the pintle handle. I fired from the prone, ripping off bursts that dug earth but yards away. A white rag on a stick suddenly came up. I stopped firing. A hatless Chinese soldier with hands-up climbed out of his foxhole; another in a brown quilted uniform followed. I kept the weapon in their face. Both crouched coming up slope. A trailing infantry man took the POWs. Warren lobbed a grenade into the enemy hole. Only black acrid smoke emerged.

  "Pull back," ordered Able's platoon leader.

  Once back to the MLR, immense fire power immersed the battle area, its fury and violence hurling stones, splinters and shrapnel like a volcano hurled lava. The air smelled of sulfite thick as smoke above

Gary, Indiana. I didn't envy the enemy. I heard a buzz, a reciprocating sound increasing in volume. I ducked as dirt spewed a gusher. I looked at my legs. They were there. So was a huge hunk of embedded metal. My entrenching tool handle was cut through. Catching breath, I exchanged my stump for a full handled shovel. I'd have to dig a hole out there.

"Saddle up!"

I mounted the tripod. Riflemen stood, their weapons at the ready. The putt, putt of our mortars turned on as if a switch were thrown.

"Move out!"

Mortars to our front blasted earth high. The stone wall was down. Artillery worked demolition up the ridgeline. Able's men formed a scything skirmish line under cover of 1st and 2nd section four machine guns hammering the check point. From the angry hill came a heavy pouring of automatic fire. Burp guns, machine-guns. There was grazing fire flying everywhere.

"In the shell hole," Warren ordered. "Fire on the checkpoint."

I flipped the tripod into the shell hole. We set up. I ran a burst across a horizontal trench. Torres' gun joined. Our skirmishers moved forward. We shifted fire at the safety point just above the heads of riflemen. They overran the check point. We moved up. There were shell holes everywhere, bunkers bashed in, trench walls down. Chinese were mangled into grotesque poses. It was a morgue. I didn't pay attention to the dead. I loosened dirt from trench walls to cover human parts before I dug in to cover Able's leapfrog. Chogie bearers, Korean civilians, came up with supplies. They carried the wounded back.

    Able jumped off. I fired bursts of six! No return fire? Had the enemy pulled back to Hill 598, hopefully to Hill 1062? If so, the last check point would be a cake-walk. To do it, Shoemaker ran us down slope 30 feet into a trench. It ran the horizontal length of the checkpoints. We could keep our heads down. Enemy on the ridgeline hadn't targets of us, but those on Hill 598 did. Mortar rounds walked our way. Zinging shrapnel crooned.

    We set up to view the top of the objective. There was an ominous silence. Able 3rd jumped off and I fired, ripping apart sand bags on trench lips. Riflemen fired as they advanced. Tracers looked like hot fireflies pricking the sky where the trench wound like a snake upward to a formidable bunker. Our tracers barely cleared heads to suppress enemy fire. It didn't the grenades flipping out from defensive positions. Sounds from various caliber weapons played a deadly symphony. It grew louder and fiercer every step of the skirmish line. To move forward was a plunge into the jaws of crocodiles. I threw in a heavy flood of rounds but the hosts of the hilltop hurled back a mad swell of automatic fire. Grenades plugged the tide of onrushing infantry. They hustled for cover behind boulders, in shell holes, going no further uphill.

    Across the sweeping ridgeline, Able's PFC Michael Hibser, looking a hump-backed, flung himself recklessly upward toward death on the crest. Leaping trenches, jumping boulders, he dashed with a flame thrower's liquid in triple cylinders on his back. He carried a nozzle in hand to squirt fire into the bunker. Like posing for a photograph, he stood at the enemy's gun port amidst exploding grenades and flashing muzzles. He aimed his nozzle to let its flame free. It trickled like a faucet leak. He tried again. It didn't even trickle. Our shooting erupted in a frenzy at the spectacle of Hibser ripping the flame thrower from his back to escape down a defile from a hail of lead and grenade fragments. Then he fell, plunging downward, rolling into a deep abyss. Awe struck, we momentarily ceased firing.

    Waves of tracers resumed the chafing of the crest bunker. It was a strange block of lumpy construction on a windy, treeless pinnacle that lurched out at all who gave challenge for mastery of the hill. Its soldiers swept our trench lines with their own lead in response. We exchanged fire forever, but the assaulters stayed pinned.

    Strikingly dominating the ridgeline was another humpback soldier. The gait was familiar. Hibser? He'd return with the flames of hell splashing an inferno of liquid that forced the enemy from their gun holes. Finished, he flung his flaming instrument down. He fell, rolling down the sharp slope like a prostrate log. The bunker erupted with Vesuvius' shriek across the crest. We felt the shock waves in the commo, "communication," trench. Hibser's heroism inspired the 3rd platoon. They charged, loosening hell on the resistance.

    Any surviving Chinese who could bug, did. They dashed from fighting holes, running down a long slanting hill that looked like a finger from the back of a hand. Targets of opportunity! I shifted fire from the crest into their flight, slicing bursts of six, cutting into them until there were but three who dared to chance the accuracy of my weapon. My blood high, one by one, I ripped each with a burst of six. A second burst into each body rolling down slope settled it for all eternity. I wasn't fighting for God, Country or family! I was fighting for Mike Hibser, George Shoemaker, Dean Warren, Hartland Clouse, William Bouton, my squad, my section, for Able. I was fighting for my buddies! Had the enemy surrendered than run to fight again, I wouldn't have cut short their futures.

"Move up," ordered Shoemaker. "Dig in where the trench turns up to the hilltop. Get ready for counterattack. Love and How machine-guns are on the way to relieve by 1730 hours. By the way, Red, Dog Six sends congratulations for cutting down those bugging gooks."

I wasn't too enthralled. Rather, I shuddered over the coming of relief, knowing arithmetical time changed to geometrical proportions on a newly conquered hill. My gun crew cleared the bend in the commo trench of its dead Chinese. There was considerable room on the back slope to place bodies out of our field of fire. They weren't very big men by our physical standards, but it didn't take size to pull a trigger. It took fortitude. From the fight they put up, there had been plenty of fortitude. We dug with fury. If we had to defend this dreadful precinct, we would construct a battlement for the duration of the war. We dug deeply into the bank, opening a fire port, pulled logs from bunkers, set up joists and crossed them on top with other logs. A grass mat went to the top of the roof. Sandbags were filled and double layered above, around the firing port, behind us. It offered cover absent a direct hit. They were never heard, just suffered.

Chogie bearers flooded the trench, dropping off cans of water, fragmentation grenades, boxes of ammo, bandoleers, combat rations. They left 10 ammo cans before they moved up the trench line toward the burned out remnants of the fortified crest. I was refilling my canteen when a Chinese whistle blew. It was their turn to try the hill. A ghostly stomping rushed down the trench line behind my position. The fearful faces I saw weren't the enemy, but Chogies. I watched a fleeing fold of sheep lashing at one another to beat their way off the hill. Diemer hopped up, grunted and bolted down the trench tailing the last bugout. I blinked. Just when the whole squad had attributed a touch of stability to the mustiest soldier in the 35th Regiment, 25th Infantry Division, he'd bugged-out. A burp gun chirped. M-1 rifles popped, a light .30 caliber machine-gun cut in. Torres and I arched tracers. We were unmerciful on the enemy's infantry coming up behind their mortars' impacts. Shells clobbered both sides of the trench.

Above the din, cries came from serrated flesh. "Litter bearer! Where are the litter bearers?"

"Bugged out."

"They be coming," said Diemer, voice piercing the smoky air, his M 2 carbine, its bayonet fixed, pointed at the backs of Chogies. They went about their work as inscrutably as their guard. I was conscience stricken thinking Diemer a bug-out in the face of the enemy. He was a heroic riddle without a single clue.

The enemy skirmishers broke off. It was late in the day and night was more favorable. They'd return in the dark, but not on my shift! Love and How were up the trench line to relieve. I'd made the heat of the day. If prayer slipped my mind during battle, it wasn't anymore. Hymns swam in the veins of my brain like Tarzan in a jungle river.

Who would have thought, returning to the MLR from battle, that pulling night guard duty and digging trenches the next day was so satisfying? How could it be otherwise when Mike Hibser, numbered among Able's 16 casualties, lived and the truce talks resumed? Negotiators were working on an armistice line. Our side wanted the present battle line, a line down the middle of no man's land between us and them, both sides pulled back creating a demilitarized zone, DMZ. Back slope rumors told the enemy hadn't rejected the idea. Great news if it went into effect instantly. Bad news if the talking over a DMZ went on as long as it took the sides at the beginning of the truce talks to agree on what to talk about in the first place. There was more bad news. A stateside newspaper poll reported American civilians thought the Korean War utterly useless! Useless?

"Hear this," said Shoemaker. "150 Chinks tried the hill. Love and How beat them off but have 26 casualties. Charley 3 and 3rd section will relieve them at 0700 hours. We go where Charley goes."

If so, why hadn't the 1st section gone out with Able? No matter!! Out we went through the long trench, heads down. The enemy fired flat trajectory 76 millimeter shells to open the commo trench and expose us to direct fire. A round whistled in. Another crashed close, the section chewing trench mud.

"Medic!" Warren lifted Griscones' head but all Doc Davidson could do was call Chogie bearers.

Private Griscones' second day of battle and his life, was over.

  We continued through the trench under fire until our counter fire slowed it. Return to the horseshoe bend on the crest was a run through a punch press. There was a fury of red, black, green, blue and purple clouds rolling up from the mount. If I wondered where hell was, I'd located it. Love had strung barbed wire. Enemy casualties hung on it. Others laid like flat pavement stones. A Chinaman on the reverse lip of the trench groaned. There wasn't much of a human being remaining. His left arm was shattered; its tourniquet had lost its purpose. Legs were mangled. A bloody face opened one eye. His right hand formed a finger pistol against his temple. A plea for execution. I wouldn't do it. A rifleman came up the trench. The nod from the man of China to the man of America translated to chivalry. The GI set his M-1 on the bloody chest, its muzzle under the chin. The Chinaman's finger was inserted on the trigger. He pulled it.

  The shells fell with rain drop frequency as if self-execution rendered clouds. The hillside turned into a blazing inferno. Mouths caught more dirt than entrenching tools. I remounted the gun in the bunker I'd left behind. Its roof beams sagged, but would take a close hit. We hurried to sand bag the forward aperture. Two rounds came in, a 10 or 20 second interval, then two more. The time between rounds lessened. More incoming cracked the earth. I pulled the tripod back so the gun wasn't protruding through the aperture like a lightning rod. The barrage was incessant, flashes of orange casting a Halloween tinge.

The unending day was unmerciful. A crushing explosion rocked the floor of the trench. I felt asphyxiated by the fumes, demented from concussion. Soldiers moved through the trench at a crawl or squatted low as frogs. A massive convulsion near the crest rolled a huge bolder down slope across the trench line, a near miss from crushing. A deafening roar echoed from the left side of the perimeter. Some ears wouldn't hear.

They were on high ground and had us plotted to the square root working on violent relocation. The sound of ruptured shells sent an echo of a rumbling thunderstorm. Nature itself wasn't up to getting me out from under my steel pot when billowing debris fell. The ground shivered the gun's ammo belt. 3rd rifle squad leader Sergeant Ronald Smith kept squeezing off rounds as if back in Florida at a known distance range. Not even incoming thick as leaves in late fall phased him. Other heads stayed down. The thunder of incoming swelled with no crescendo evident. I prayed at every impact. I prayed for the guys in the section, in Smith's squad, in Charley 3, in the Raiders, for Griscones, for myself. If the fires of hell were at the trench bend, we were committed prematurely!

A thunderclap flung me backwards as if a limp rag. I smacked the far trench wall, staring at the swirling, mushrooming cloud. All was silent. I looked at the gun hole. Its roof had disappeared, sand bags bled. My gun was a twisted end-iron. Clouse bled from the nose but was alive. Bouton too. Was he hollering? I wondered where his words went. My field jacket was splashed with blood. I moved my hands looking for the wound. I couldn't find it. Nothing hurt as much as my temples. Something had hit them hard as a sledge hammer. I felt my ears. Present! Nothing leaked. My blood? Looking around, I saw Charley's Corporal Michael Petruska down, his radio smashed; and Private Jean Christie down, his Browning Automatic Rifle, BAR, on the trench floor. Both were shattered. Christie's clothes had the color of dark brown hay in flames. Beneath the pall of a sulfite cloud, a snowy color crept over his countenance even as medic, Corporal Eugene 'Doc' Doyle, worked a vein. Petruska's first aid packet's whiteness changed to the colors of autumn leaves.

 I seethed with anger, sorrow, thankfulness. Anger at the enemy, sorrow over the loss of Griscones, Christie and Petruska, thankfulness for survival. I prayed for the repose of their souls, for quick recoveries by the wounded, for my aching head, for the whistling in my ears to tune down, and next breath, gratitude for the bunker roof, the survival of Clouse and Bouton.

 Cautious helmets oozed out of fighting holes like newly hatched turtles out of sea sand. I realized we were being pulled out. Dead and wounded, equipment and ammo gathered, we worked back down the trench while scores of anvils split and hissed. The quick flash of a blue green light led the train of noise. The ground jerked us around as if on railroad tracks waiting for the train to run us over.

 *

 In those gun pits all wild with wrath, soldiers who'd never met before or would meet again except on the battlefield, fired artillery, mortars, machine-guns and rifles to wound and kill for a hilltop between lines.

It was madness when there was talk of a DMZ! Madness to fight for the next hilltop for there was no end. Across the next valley rose a chain of higher peaks clear through to China, Manchuria and into Siberia. Was the well being of the Eight Army more assured on one high peak as opposed to another a thousand yards ahead or back? What was in the minds of those who instructed the truce talkers?

     Griscones, Christie and Petruska were dead. Able, Dog, Love, How, Charley and the Cacti Raiders, absent the killed in action with graves registration and the wounded at the aid stations, were back where they started. All movement ceased on the long ridgeline. Even the enemy didn't stay on it. Combat was a tree of bitterness grown from evil roots.

OPERATION CACTI OFFICIAL REPORTS

On 24 October 1951, a tent city was set up at Panmunjon. On 25 October United Nations' Truce Negotiators Major General Henry L. Hodes and Rear Admiral Arleigh A. Burke submitted to Communists' Major General Lee Sang Cho and Major General Hsieh Fang a proposal for a demilitarized zone based on the line of contact traced on a map. On 26 October the Communists countered with a map of their own. <u>Truce Tent and Fighting Front</u>, pages 113 - 116, <u>by Walter G. Hermes</u>, Center of Military History, United States Army, 1988. On 25 October 1951, a Regimental Task force composed of a platoon of infantry and a platoon of tanks was assigned a diversionary attack mission in conjunction with a limited objective attack by elements of the 2nd ROK Division, the unit on the right flank of the 35th Infantry. The mission of the patrol was to secure objective CACTI, CT675436, determine enemy disposition, destroy enemy positions, take captive enemy personnel, and to seize or destroy enemy material. Four rocky precipices which dominate the principal ridgeline extending to the North of the 1st Battalion's sector constituted the objective. The patrol was composed of the 3rd platoon of Company "C" 89th Tank Battalion and the 3rd platoon of "A" Company, 1st Battalion. <u>Lt. Col. Thomas W. Woodyard Jr, Regimental Commander.</u>, Headquarters, 35th Infantry Regiment, 25th Infantry Division, Command Report # 11, 15 November 1951.

    On 25 October 1951, "A" Company jumped off on a limited objective attack, their objective being vicinity CT677426. Heavy opposition was encountered within 300 yards and the lead elements of "A" Company returned to friendly MLR. After another preparation of artillery and mortar fire was placed on the objective and "A" Company jumped off again at 1105 hours. This attempt was very successful and "A" Company secured their objective at approximately 1515 hours. Eleven prisoners were taken and actual count showed 20 enemy KIA and many wounded. In this operation, flame throwers were used very advantageously. "L" Company, 35th RCT was attached to this Battalion and commencing at 1700 hours relieved "A" Company on their objective. "A" Company returned to position on friendly MLR. During the night, "L" Company repulsed a company sized counter-attack. "L" Company suffered 26 casualties but succeeded in holding the ground.

At 1000 hours, 27 October 1951, "C" Company and the Raider Platoon relieved "L" Company on position. "L" Company reverted to parent organization. "C" Company received over 500 reported rounds of artillery and mortar fire on position. Due to the excessive amount of enemy fire received on position, it was necessary to withdraw "C" Company to friendly MLR. <u>Major Homer J. Butler, Regimental S-3.</u>, Command Report # 11. On 27 October 1951, one reinforced platoon of "C" Company relieved "L" Company at CT678425. During the relief and thereafter, "C" Company received heavy artillery and mortar fire resulting in three friendly KIA and 12 friendly MIA. "C" Company withdrew to MLR on order at 1900 hours. <u>Captain John Amaker, Regimental S-2.</u>, Command Report # 11.

OPERATION MESABI

The poncho covering the elbow entry to Dog's 1st machine gun bunker swung in as Joe ROK entered to relieve me from guard duty. "Want you at warming bunker," he hollered.

He had to holler. My head hurt so after the incoming on hill 440, my brain was in a cloud that hung over me. In it were ghosts shrieking and a heavenly crescent glittering with diamonds under a glowing rainbow. I said not a word to my squad leader, Warren, about the screaming noises or imaginary scenery within my skull. On my way up the commo trench to back slope I figured, once out of the Army, I'd have to get a hearing aid. I envisioned a long trumpet like the types I'd seen in Saturday movie matinee cartoons.

On entering the warming bunker I saw Truscott reading the Book of Mormon; LaSapio as if frozen to an ammo box chair; Gzregorek with spiritless eyes; Baldy Heideman's head in his hands and Private Lamont Geiger, face sullen as a kicked cat, prone on the bench above the buried Chink. (The body, first buried by GI incoming, was buried again under the floor when it's arms were uncovered). Geiger had been recently transferred to 35th Regiment's Dog machine guns from the 24th Regiment, black soldiers under command of white officers. President Harry Truman had ordered a stop to such segregation.

Judging by the manifest depression, we'd been ordered out on another attack! My gut tightened to rope. "When and where?" I asked.

"Too loud," Truscott yelled.

My sound was outdoing the everlasting whistling, roaring and hissing inside my ears. I was losing control of my sense of hearing. I cupped my ears that he'd know.

He hollered. "1062."

"Lord have mercy." Survival on the highest hill was minuscule.

2nd gun's gunner Torres came in crossing himself as if entering a cathedral. The squad's men not on guard duty followed. Dog Six, Company commander, followed them. Shoemaker sounded 'attention' and we came to it, then 'at ease' by Dog Six. He started moving about like a cheerleader, all tuned up about destroying the enemy and taking the high ground. Hearing him was listening to a static radio. "Attention!" He left. "At ease!"

Shoemaker howled. "Here's the word. On D-day, November 1, (1951), the first battalion attacks with the 14th Regiment. Next the 35th's second and third battalions and the 27th Regiment attack. The brass call it Operation Mesabi. Oh yea, stack your gear. We go off line tomorrow at 0500 hours. That's all." No one in the section was late to drag butt off the MLR to the Kumhwa valley even knowing those same butts would soon be put in 1062's sling. Approaching our field kitchen, cook, smiling, watched us come in, our eyes dimmed headlights. "I got corn on the cob for that new recruit from Pennsylvania. Where is he?"

"Killed in action," Warren answered.

Cook's eyes misted when he put the corn back into the pot. He stirred its hot water a time or two, turned and walked from the feeding line to the cook tent.

A black soldier came out of the kitchen. His eyes opened wide at the sight of Geiger. "You as big as Soldier's Field in Chicago, man," hissed the long and lean soldier with the look of a GI who had failed the short arm inspection. You from Deuce-four Dog or How?"

"How Company," Geiger said. "Who you?"

"Leroy Goins," he answered. "Was in Mike. Talked to get honor guard back to Division but some rear echelon crud sitting around like he always do, shipped me to this line outfit. No telling them nothing. CO put me in the 3rd section. Cook put me on KP 'til you came off the hill."

"Get some hot coffee and forget it," Geiger suggested. "You're with me." The cold of late October numbed fingers. Winter gloves helped. Waiting on D-day, the outfit pitched pup-tents, readied gear and ran problems with tank units to prepare for the assault. Tankers in our chow line huffed about box mines that Chinks were known to slide so deeply under roads mine sweepers couldn't find all of them. Engineers answered that if they turned their sensors up high it registered on everything down there. If they dug every time they would never be ready by D-day. I wished engineers would lead infantry up 1062.

The CO entered the mess tent where his platoon leaders, section sergeants and squad leaders were slugging coffee. "This is the plan in brief. The 14th Regiment leads and seizes objectives De Soto, Pontiac and Olds on line Duluth. The Turks take objective Packard. The 27th Regiment on the left seizes Reo, Buick, and Auburn on line Duluth. 3d Division's 7th Regiment blocks. H-hour is 0615. The 35th stays in blocking but first battalion prior to darkness moves up, ties in with the 14th and displays all air panels."

Someone raised a question. "Are the truce talks off?"

"No, but if the Commies were talking to end the fighting no purpose would be served to attack. They aren't. It's less costly to attack now than give them time to build up. Eighth Army's Scotch Six wants the Iron Triangle. We'll attack northeast and cut off the North Korean forces. Then the enemy will talk like they mean it to end the fighting. The truce talks have been used by the Commies as a tool in preventing their defeat and the moment is near when that will end. Able Company hits the road at 0645, then Charley, Dog and Baker follow. By 1400 hours on D-day, Charley Company will relieve the 14th's George Company and assume full responsibility for their zone." The waiting for November 1st ended. I remembered last night back home was Halloween and the whole of the world of the supernatural now rested, but what about the natural? My sense of touch worked because I felt the morning's biting cold but where was our outgoing? There was a grand silence as if Kumhwa were a seminary dormitory where even the Prefect was quiet.

"Hear this," LaSapio yelled, waking up the pup tents, "the attack's postponed 24 hours."

We took the delay with a lot of discomfort. There were just so many times an infantryman could get himself up for an assault, particularly when a rumor passed among us the Commies might again talk truce, but in a place called Panmunjon. Not much credence was given it, as a truce took pressure off them while they keep our POWs and built up their forces.

That night we found sleep on the ground hard to come by. The smell from my duck down sleeping bag was of sweat and breath so foul I was suffocating myself with the odor of fright. When a scream rent the air my zipper caught up. I had visions of some infiltrator killing me in my fart sack and my obituary reading that I had died with the odor of sanctity, that odor, according to the Lives of the Saints read to seminarians at mealtimes, that arose from saints after forty days of penitence in a locked cell. I got the zipper free and pulled on my snopacs.

"Look at dawn cracking," LaSapio hollered. "Come out of the pup tents and feel the cold wind on your face. Attack's off! We're alive three more days." He was as happy as a bartender in New York on St. Patrick's Day, and skipping around like a little girl at hop-scotch. "Look at them chimney pipes on the mess tents. Their smoke's twisting Indian signs. Sun's coming up like a plate of gold. Get up! Hot chow's on the stove!"

We used the three days to train recruits how to dig a good fighting hole, to reinforce a bunker, to tell the sounds of incoming. We taught perimeter defense, the sounds of night guard, the dangers of mine fields, the superior fire power of a tight unit. We were ready for 1062 on the morning of D-day plus 4.

"Wake up, Red," LaSapio shouted. "Wake up 3rd section. Fall on your knees in this clean snow. We got praying to do."

"What's up? Another three days?"

"Operation Mesabi is postponed without a

date," he hooted. "We ain't going against 1062. Truce tent's talking. In a week or two there's going to be a line between us and them with no crossing the line; but we still have to rotate units on the MLR. Each battalion goes on line for two weeks then a week in reserve. We go back up on line November 14."

There was prayer in the snow on that bizarre day. No one would be killed or wounded in action on 1062.

WALKING THE DOG

The air sang as the eighty-two millimeter mortar round shattered earth near our machine gun emplacement on Kumhwa, North Korea's Main Line of Resistance.

"Keep your head down," I screamed at Private Sergio LaSapio. The breath broke from his mouth as I pulled him back into the bunker by his fatigue shirt twisting it around his throat like a hangman's noose.

Two more rounds came in, their sounds suddenly sinking like stones into the sea.

I said with urgency, "Always keep your head down when the Chinks are walking the dog. You'll get hit if you peek. Incoming that sounds 'swoosh' is usually far enough away to be safe, but if you hear a swoosh, hit the ground anyway. If it's a 'swish', it's up your nose with dog droppings." LaSapio might have viewed me as a vulture on carrion when I illustrated by drawing my fingers as if they were knives across a throat. "Chinks kill more GIs with shrapnel than rounds, so no peeking. Just hide in the hole when it's incoming. Time enough to look when they lift fire!"

LaSapio knew eloquence when he heard it.

COOTIE HUNT

Hunching down while going from bunker to bunker, Staff Sergeant Dean Warren said to his men, "Cootie hunt on the back slope."

All but the two left on guard duty took him up on it. Those of the machine gun squad who hunted for lice got a break in the evening from line routine. In addition to looking for lice bedded down in fatigues, we shot the breeze and rested sore backs from digging trenches.

Warren hated lice. His Grandpa called them cooties during the first world war thirty-three years back and had to live with them in the trenches. They didn't have modern cootie powder then. We were ordered to hunt and destroy, to powder seams even without sight of a critter, especially Private Earl Diemer who was believed to carry the mother house of lice. He ferried a boat load and remained the headwater of all the squad's cooties.

I was first up the communication 'commo' trench to the reverse slope and found an ammo box to sit on while I took off my fatigue shirt to check its seams for lice. I saw none. Warren and the others came out of the commo trench removing their shirts. They spread out around me sitting on rocks and ammo boxes to start searches. I next took off my undershirt to check it out but the evening air was so chilly from the wind off the north mountains the freckles on my pale skin blanched. I looked a TB consumptive. I checked the undershirt but found no cooties. As the wind was too biting to sit long without it, I pulled it back on.

"Don't you have to pick lice, gunner?" LaSapio asked.

"No! I don't know why it is but no one in the gun hole has lice."

He gave me a wide eyed look. "I'm finding a whole lot." He held his shirt while his fingernails bisected the caught culprits. "Got more powder, Sergeant?" There was already so much louse powder around his undershirt, LaSapio looked a swan with ghostly shoulders.

"Here's another packet." Warren handed it over.

LaSapio opened it and slapped it all over. A cloud of floury white spluttered like a mist in a lowland. He sighed in exasperation, then said, "I forgot my toilet paper." Stepping out of the mist, he pulled on his fatigue shirt. It waved behind him as he jogged up the slope into the commo trench. Quickly back, his shirt buttoned up and toilet paper in hand, he ventured, the first of the squad to do so, the fifty feet down slope to drop a note of welcome within the new straddle crapper. Privacy was afforded by shelter halfs. He assumed the position just when something exploded fifteen yards down slope.

"What was that?" Warren said from the prone. He picked himself up. "Sounded like a Chink concussion grenade. LaSapio must have kicked it loose. Look!"

LaSapio had leapt from the straddle crapper as if pole vaulting. When he landed, his feet were hung up in his trousers. He somersaulted and rolled like a log. Gravity had him by the butt. He chuted off the hillside disappearing from view.

I took off after him. Others too. We saw him sprawled on a rock overhang wrapped in brush, face as purple as the distant mountains. When we reached him, his shirt and undershirt were torn away.

"Is he okay?" Warren asked, kneeling beside me.

Corporal Wilbur 'Doc' Davidson was there to examine arms, legs, ribs. He felt for his pulse. "Nothing seems broken but what's around his neck?"

"I'll be!" Warren said. "A necklace of beads? Why is he wearing a necklace? He wasn't when delousing. Must have put it on when he went for the toilet paper." Warren studied it. "What is it, Red?"

I answered, "What you call a necklace is a Roman Catholic Rosary. Usually one carries it in a pocket. LaSapio must like to wear it."

Doc mused, "Maybe LaSapio thinks it an ancient Roman insecticide."

RATS

A rock fell from the log roof of the bunker. Above my bunk was Oscar, a rabbit-sized rat, nibbling on communication wire. Our phone line was off limits. I got out my entrenching tool. Its blade would bisect the creepy thing if I could lure him from the shelter of the logs. From a C-ration can, I flipped a hunk of cheese and bacon on the floor. Oscar's eyes beaded and nose twitched but he didn't give a hoot for cheese. Packages with home cookies were more to his taste. I was offended. What the Army said was good enough for its front line soldiers should suit a rodent.

Having no cookies, perhaps there was something around, another bait, more to Oscar's taste. Someone had charcoal heated hamburgers in a c-ration can full of thick grease and left it. A lump of the stuff might attract the inky critter. He watched as I gently set out a piece. As I did, I kept my entrenching tool hidden behind me. Nothing happened. The creature was finicky. An officer?

Other rats ran the rafters, eyeing the hamburger. I readied the entrenching tool but it appeared as if Oscar told the bait was his, hissing a warning to ignore it. Instead the rat pack took to fighting. Oscar fell from the log rafters like an enormous black rain drop. I beheaded him. A second rodent fell. I sliced through its gut. Others cascaded. I flailed like a wild man; swinging a rifle butt at one, tossing an ammo can that crushed another. A grizzly sight! Carnage! It looked as if the inside of the sleeping bunker had taken a Chink 82 millimeter mortar round.

I'd baited. I'd killed. I cleaned up the gore. I scooped rat parts off the floor and walls onto burning charcoal in the ammo can, cremating remains, scattering them to a northerly wind.

TRUCE TALKS

"Here." Private Joe ROK, siting ramrod straight on his cot, the look in his wide eyes one of disgust, beckoned Warren to come over.

He left the prone on his cot to sit down beside me on my cot. I said, "What's up?"

Because Section Sergeant George Shoemaker's poker game was off, and he was dozing, Joe ROK hissed, "Havee no truce now. Nam Il of Imun Gun losee face to Chinese General."

"What did Joe say?" I asked Warren.

"No truce?" Warren didn't whisper. "What does the loss of face by a North Korean General to a General of the Chinese Communist Forces mean to us? What did that have to do with the truce talks?"

Joe ROK continued to hiss with edginess. "Chinkee soldier givee matches to Nam Il, but Chinkee matches never burn. Nam Il can't light cigarette so usee GI lighter. Chinkee General see! So Nam Il throwee GI lighter out window, walkee out on truce talk to showee scorn for GI. No truce!"

"No truce over a GI cigarette lighter?" Warren was very loud.

Shoemaker sat straight up on his cot and glared, pale as a drained corpse.

Warren's words out did the hissing in my ears.

Whether or not Joe ROK was correct the squad leader felt he had to try to calm his section sergeant. "The rumor I heard Shoe, was someone walked out of the talks, not over a GI cigarette lighter, but over the dividing line to be drawn between Armies. Commies want the line on the 38th parallel, not north of it."

"We're twenty miles north of the 38th since June (1951). The hills here are no easier to attack or defend and don't look different than the south. So why stay north?"an experienced infantryman questioned. "Let's get back to the 38th and end this stupid war. Too many good men have gone down to enemy fire, and for what? Another hill?" His concern up, he paused to catch a breath. "What else did you hear?"

"Nothing that you probably don't know, Shoe. Like the truce talks have broken off two or three times already. One time because the Commies claimed we dropped a flare over Kaesong or we bombed it. We said they faked it. Still, they're switching sites. I did hear by way of the mess tent that General Van Fleet said if the ROKs on line are hit by the Chinks and GIs have to start fighting again we'll be an eager army."

"Eager?" Shoemaker said. "The general forgets the enemy. I remember when the Chinks came at us in April. Their weapons squads carried machine guns on bamboo poles slung from the shoulders of two of them. There wasn't fear in them." His face redden as he spoke. He began rocking on his cot. "When the Turks were hit hard we were sent up on the double to relieve them. We had artillery support and it left pieces of Chinks everywhere. Still they came jumping bodies cutting us off. We fought our way out bringing our casualties with us. Some of our wounded took shrapnel two or three times but we got them out. We'd pull back and have to do it all over again and again, clear back to Line Golden near Seoul. We were dug in there but the Chinks jumped our barbwire, ran into our mine fields, booby traps, napalm drums, white phosphorus rounds, everything to get at us. They couldn't do it. My front looked like a civil war battlefield. No! We won't be no eager army."

Shoe rolled onto his back, then over to the right side and reached for his helmet. It was pulled on his head as if he needed protection from memories of Line Golden.

I followed the gist of their discussion. I wished it were different in the truce tent. Men at Kaesong and Panmunjon argued over lines for troops to patrol and defend, while politicians in Washington D. C., and Peking argued the same topics but with a different intent: avoidance of political embarrassment. Politicians, ours and theirs, willfully, knowingly and deliberately ordered the continuation of the fighting. They were the real killers from a distance.

I prayed for a quick resumption of the truce talks.

A CHRISTMAS SONG

On Kumhwa's earthly MLR with unearthly weather the days of late fall were highlighted by incoming and outgoing but no infantry assaults. During Thanksgiving chow the wind howled and sleet bit through our parkas, its shock demoralizing chow hounds. Rumors flew thick as peas and frozen gravy in mess kits that the truce would be a fact on December 27, 1951.

If it weren't so, how many would have courage squeezed into cranberry sauce?

If it were so, why had Private Norb Grezorek composed this Christmas song?

"Kumhwa night, lonely night;
Naught is calm, set gun sight.
Round yon table in Panmunjon
Tired men would war abandon.
Sleep under the truce's spell;
Die when the Chinese shell."

POW

    The first seven months I was in Korea I was an Army Private; a gunner for six of those months on a water cooled heavy 30 caliber machine gun. In mid-February 1952, Dog Company's Commanding Officer, 'CO', deemed PFC James F. 'Red' Walsh, worthy of Corporal stripes. I was glad of it for I needed the extra money seeing how a pack of GI issued cigarettes that came with the c-rations was no longer economically sufficient to trade for a can of 3.2 beer. About that time, the CO of the 35th Regiment deemed the 1st Battalion worthy to relieve the Turk Battalion on the main line of resistance, 'MLR', on the Punchbowl, a series of hills so tall and round, the valley they surrounded bore a remarkable resemblance to a monstrous beaker.

    The winds over the Punchbowl were born in Siberia, teenage with passage south through Manchuria; adult in North Korea. Tales told by GIs who'd pulled the winter of 1950 - 1951 lingered in my memory. The troops of all nations suffered terrible privations, particularly in bitterly cold sleet storms. Cold was intense, snow deep. The wind howled as it bit through fatigues during the short days and long icy nights on the bare hills while a soldier lay on frozen ground. The sudden shock of Korea's winter demoralized many outfits that tried to stand and fight the invading Chinese of November 1950. The winter of 1951-1952 wasn't different. Korea was an earthly place with an unearthly weather.

    The climb of Dog's 1st Section of Heavy machine guns up the hill with full equipment was in bitter cold. The higher we labored, the sharper the bite of the winter wind and the cuts from flakes of razor edged snow. Staff Sergeant Dean Warren pulled the 1st squad up and into abandoned enemy bunkers to rest, but sent me to locate the Turks' positions. I couldn't speak their language, but so what! All that was needed was to find swarthy looking soldiers in GI fatigues who couldn't speak ours.

    The ground I walked was hard as granite. Snow was accumulating on top of accumulation. Fingers and toes, other parts of me were very cold, no matter the training on prevention of frostbite. I'd learned blood circulation at very low temperatures was greatly retarded, extremities susceptible to frostbite or immersion foot. So, over my OD wool gloves, I wore GI machine gun mittens, especially designed for gunners. The index finger on both hands had covering separate from the other digits. I could pull the trigger with the left index finger and traverse and search with the right. I'd made sure my shoepacs, (we called them snowpacs), fitted. Though the snowpacs' rubber foot and oiled leather top was designed to keep the foot dry, they did little about sweaty feet. That was supposedly handled by not blousing trousers into the boot tops. If trousers weren't bloused, it was supposed to allow evaporation of sweat through the top of the boot. Most of us buttoned the field trousers around the ankle outside the boot, as suggested, to allow for evaporation. Still, my feet sweated, so I carried extra wool socks to change where ever there was some lack of cold. A rarity climbing North Korea's hilltops! The hood of my windproof parka was pulled over the helmet which sat on a heavy winter cap with ear flaps.

They were down. The parka was worn over a field jacket over an olive drab, 'OD', sweater over a fatigue shirt over an OD shirt over long johns on the upper torso and water proof field trousers over fatigue pants over OD wool trousers over long johns (without booties) on the lower torso. Such layers of clothing were intended to hold in body heat, but up on the Punchbowl, it wasn't working very well.

    I came across a tank, motor humming. It looked a giant tortoise with snowy hair. To drive and tow it up on the rough cut road a hundred feet from the crest of the mountain was no easy engineering feat. My down sleeping bag, (I went no where in winter's mountains without it), was in a waterproof, windproof case. I rolled it out, slid it under the tank, climbed in, boots and all but the helmet, seeking momentary refuge under the tortoise's warm belly. Reheated and regenerated, I moved up and came upon the Turks. One, a Sergeant, spoke our language. Sort of! Together we were able to complete the relief.

    We moved into bunkers that looked like infected warts. There was little evidence of digging. The Turks must have broken so many entrenching tools in ground frozen solid that they settled for cutting down back slope trees to build tall bunkers on the forward slope.

    Relief completed, Dog Company's 3rd Section of machine guns was on the Punchbowl MLR, living, if it could be called living, in the dead of a howling winter. We heated the bunker with charcoal burning inside an empty machine gun ammo metal box. To remedy our exposed situation, my gun crew and I appropriated picks and worked the bone cold days, chiseling into the earth from within the confines of the bunker. As if we were in a sinking ship, the profile of the bunker dropped lower and lower. We wanted it less visible than a sore thumb on a boxer. Over time, communication trenches were dug to connect fighting holes and safe passage to the reverse slope. The Chinese worked as tirelessly boring tunnels, digging out caves and trenches.

    Although no truce had been agreed between armies, the exchange of fire diminished, and with it casualties, a welcomed benefit. Yet Officers, ours and theirs far removed from the MLR, insisted sniping not be forgotten. A well aimed round from a 50 caliber machine gun reminded infantrymen, whatever his nationality, a head exposed was subject to an eternal headache. Then fate intervened. Our sniper answered sick call and missed duty. The day passed without our side sniping. Their side didn't snipe the next day. The IQ of one serving his nation as a foot soldier might be questioned, but not the instinct for survival pending the truce. Front line troops took advantage and declared a private truce on sniping.

    On duty in the fighting hole, I was the last guard of a very cold night. The moon was fading, the wind singing a requiem, yet dancing with inclement moods. The days were running a longer race and snow had virtually disappeared from the forward slope. The gun hole's last guard had its satisfaction. One could heat up a c-ration when daylight arrived and the night ended without any enemy crossing no man's land, the Chinese staying in their caves and tunnels. My eyes swept down slope one last time, concentrating on crevices where the dark kept secrets. I hadn't heard clinking from the c-ration cans tied on to the barbed wire. That was disturbing giving the chill wind. Were the cans caught up somehow?

Movement! Was there movement? There was! Over there, down a hundred yards. I pointed, but no one was with me to follow the point. Assistant gunner PFC Norbert Gzregorek and 1st ammo bearer PFC Carroll Truscott were dozing in the sleeping bunker. I had to be mistaken. It was nearly daylight. The enemy attacked at night, not dawn.

I doubled checked the concertina wire. Something did stir. Human? Rodent? I readied to whistle into the communication phone to alert the other soldiers on guard. Wait! Wait! I had to be sure. The whole of the infantrymen on line needed not a mistaken alert. I readied my M-2 carbine.

"Lord!" I said when two Chinks stood up in front of the concertina wire. They were a few hundred yards down slope from my fighting hole, their arms raised like branches. They weren't infiltrating but surrendering! Surrendering? If they were, I couldn't shoot them.

Was I the only one on guard? Awake? The only one on the MLR that had seen them? Those thoughts disturbed me more than two surrendering Chinamen. I couldn't leave the fighting hole to wake up Gzregorek and Truscott. I'd lose track. I whistled the communication phone for PFC Earl Diemer in the next fighting hole. I acted casually, that others listening not get aroused, asking him to wake Warren and send him to my bunker. Warren was a good man, an Iowa farmer, a top soldier, ready at a call. In the meantime, I elected to try my luck with the surrendering enemies.

Taking a chance the sniping truce hadn't been set aside and a round wouldn't swim through my brain, I stepped outside the bunker and entered the trench, raising myself up on an ammo box above the lip of the trench. I waved. They saw me and both waved back. I waved for them to come up the slope. They waved back. No movement. I waved again and again for them to come on up. They just waved back. Were they planted? I waved as if I was in the signal corps. Nothing. It was a silly surrender. They were afraid to come up the hill to our line and I didn't want to go down hill. With daylight, they were recruits for the graveyard. Their own side would bury them and pop a few rounds at me, private truce or no!

Warren showed up. "Chinks?" he said.

"Two of them surrendering." I said, pointing. "They're down to the right a few hundred yards and won't come up. I'll have to go down there to get them. Cover me, Warren." I was over the trench lip, crawling down slope before he could stop me. I stayed low, below the skyline, inch worming toward barbed wire stakes.

I heard him whistle into the commo phone, "This is Warren, Dog 3rd section, 1st machine gun. GI going out front into the barbed wire, moving down slope to take POWs. Hold fire. Pass it on."

Absent Warren's alert, my buddies in Dog and Charley Companies might have sharply reduced the size of my posterior. It was dawning on me how stupid this was, moving into barbed wire and a mind field. Thoughts of turning back played on the stage of my mind, but I'd slithered twenty-five yards down, creeping between barbed wire end poles where I'd watched rifle patrols move out on night ambushes into no-man's land. I felt Warren's eyes burning my back. Never mind, I told myself, concentrate on staying on the patrol path.

I worked down to where cattle fence barbed wire and concertina wire ended on stakes. There were the two Chinese, their hands raised, their eyes wide with surprise I'd not tripped a land mine or sprung a booby trap. I stopped and scanned the area, my carbine at the ready. No other than the two were visible. I waved them to the ground. They got down. I worked to them, frisked each, and sighed with relief I'd found no grenades, knives, weapons, just two scared Chinks. One scared GI!

I motioned for them to proceed on hands and knees. They didn't! I waved them on, they shook me off, mindful of a baseball pitcher waving off the catcher. What was the matter? I motioned my carbine threateningly, but no movement up slope. Finally, the one with the circular face moved his hands to illustrate an explosion. He feared, leading me, he'd take a wrong turn and trip a land mine. That was it. I looked up the path and saw it had a twin. I hadn't marked the path I'd traversed. 'Lord,' I silently prayed, 'have mercy on my soul. Their's too!'

Which path was the right one? No matter I was the captor, not the capturee, I'd have to lead if ever I was to return to my bunker. I once again frisked the Chinks, then crawled to the fore. My heart was still, but I led. They followed like bear cubs. I crawled from end pole to end pole, each looking a harpoon. Barbed wire sung in the wind. Once silent c-ration cans that hung everywhere were noisy as sparrows. The rising sun glared, burned, though the morning was cold.

A click! I had no blood pressure. Was a bouncing-betty under me or one of the Chinks? If one put pressure on a bouncing-betty, upon removal of the pressure, a foot or a body, the weapon sprung up from the ground and exploded, its shrapnel taking a foot, leg or life. 'Lord,' I again silently prayed for myself and the presumed Buddhists, 'have mercy on our souls.' Mongolian faces were white as mine. I looked about and saw my carbine strap hooked onto a loose strand of barbed wire. I pulled, another click. "Thank God!" was uttered with fervor.

I cradled my carbine in my arms and crawled like a sidewinder to get the devil up the hill and back into the trench line. My Mongolians hadn't hesitancy either. The lip of the trench was in sight. I beat down the urge to leap up and bolt for it in case the enemy had missed the deserters and their sniper was reenlisted. A right leg muscle cramp took that moment to twist me with agony. It was tormenting. "Lord, have mercy on my leg!"

A mushroom of flame and noise twisted the barbed wire to the left flank. White phosphorus! A quartet of incoming enemy mortar rounds followed, beating down the barbed wire. I paddled like a dog in water to the trench line and fell in. The Chinks fell on top of me. Warren arrived, his carbine leveled. The three of us didn't care. We smiled. Hands were shook.

My Chinks were POWs and safe from combat way back in the rear.

I remained on the MLR.

A few weeks later I was promoted to Staff Sergeant, its chevron three stripes above a rocker, and became Squad Leader of the 1st machine gun squad.

MASH

Orders were orders. Mine were cut for an ear examination. There was a Medical Specialist back at Division. The biting cold of Fall on the main line of resistance, MLR, wasn't the place to learn sign language; so I and my ruptured membrana tympani rode beneath the canvas on the buck boards of a bouncing deuce-by truck to the 25th Division's Mobile Army Surgical Hospital, MASH. I was worried, I admit, not so much about my hearing loss, but about not returning to Dog Company's machine gun platoon, 1st section, 1st gun squad. I'd gotten used to them and the riflemen of Charley Company's 3rd platoon, 3rd squad. We'd a close bond.

The maddened trucker had the mind to bump butts off the boards the entire route. I leaned as the truck turned onto a corrugated gravel road and roared toward a village. Suddenly the rig jerked to a shuddering stop. I rolled forward and hit the wooden rails up by the cab, my helmet falling off. Other guys piled up in a cord. I untangled from the writhing mess feeling I'd been hurled like a sock with holes that had covered its last foot. We rose unsteadily; got off and saw the problem. The front right tire had blown out. From the trucker's rabid lip flapping, fearful face and finger pointing down the road at a lone thatched hut in the village's remnants, I guessed at his worry.

"Ambush?" I said. "Unlikely. Just change the tire."

I recalled what Joe ROK, Private Im Ta Song, of my squad had told me. The rooms of his thatched hut were very small, I guessed the size of a city jail cell.

There weren't any furnishings, just mats, floors warm. In the back room was three holes, two covered by clay lids, the third opened, the kitchen with bowls for rice, a stone jar full of water; cooking pots. The holes were a ground floor stove with its fire built beneath the floor, flues running under the raised floors in the other two rooms. His Popasan, father, often sat on their home's wax paper floor meditating. Joe ROK described his Hangook Papasan as a chunk of Korea, a squat boulder rolled down from the mountain, but one who had learned to farm the mountain's side. During his six decades of life, Popasan felt the turmoil of the years. The Japanese soldiers had lined him and other Hangooks up to shout 'Banzai' when they were taken to work in a machine shop. In the long years of the Japanese occupation, Koreans in the underground, Fire Bandits, first fought the invaders, then resorted to pillaging, rape and arson. Papasan, at first, attributed his troubles to ghostly actions as taught by his ancient animistic religion. He changed his beliefs when the world around his village became a place of horror, filled with real assailants: the Imperial Japanese Army until 1945; then the Megooks from America, and, in 1950, the Imun Gun, North Korean Communists. Mamasan died when her huge jars with the family's winter supply of pickled kim-che were stolen and her only son, Im Ta Song, fled into the mountains rather than serve the North Koreans. When the Megooks returned in 1950 and chased the Imum Gun north, their war columns rushed by. Then fell the winter and with the dreadful cold came the marauding Chinese Communists over narrow mountain trails. They scattered Megooks and Hangooks like leaves before a whirlwind and, worse, they stole the family's only bullock.

Mine was a difficult walk through tents of the hospital. I saw others on stretchers and cots in long rows that never seemed to end. Some GIs were flat as shirt irons; others rigged for trapezes with pulleys, levers and ropes levitating limbs to various heights. A few troops were sitting, staring at their chameleon bandages, in awe circulating blood was taking a detour. I heard mumbling from the cots. Some of the men, log-like, were carried elsewhere, beds reclaimed by newer arrivals. There was unceasing medical staff activity. A soldier had a pretty nurse holding his hand. It was the first American woman I'd seen since July 1951. Other nurses appeared, all as beautiful, and as eager to hold GI hands like sweethearts on a front porch swing. Their tenderness and smiles brought back memories of home.

Eyes of the seriously wounded were upon me, the eyes of brave men. I walked; every muscle in my body was intact; there was no visible wound. I was where the severity of the wound brought respect, not the sightly wounded treated at a forward position and returned to their line outfit. I felt unworthy.

There was no logic to back slope respect. A line troop in a stinking outpost frozen by sleet slipping like shrapnel through a strong bitter wind who caught a flesh wound from a burp gun's bullet would be low on the dignity totem to a trucker who broke bones after his rig hit a bullock on a rear road and rolled over. This bit of logic didn't alleviate my humiliation for having a body free from apparent blemish. I wore guilt, too. Though I hadn't fired the weapon that took Charley

Company's Christie and Petruska during Operation Cacti, it was my machine gun that attracted enemy mortar fire.

I suffered an instrument poked into both ears into which the medical man peeked. Then he did a deal of talking, close and far off. I watched his lips flap like parade ground flags, but there was sound that competed with the noise within my ears! The doctor looked like an oboe and his tone was pitched high but his word's were distinguishable. For the first time since Operation Cacti there were quietly spoken words, not shouts, in my ears despite their whimsical shrieking. I knew then I wouldn't be totally deaf, though a piercing horn might forever resound within. I smiled. "I can hear you," I said. "Its been a while since I could distinguish normally spoken syllables."

I wanted out of this place. I wanted to get away from where dark haired, large eyed, slender nurses checked pulses of quiet men. I wanted to get distant from wounded faces of scorn with comets in their eyes flashing anger at the malingering worm they believed I was. I wanted to return to my unit! Probably because, by seeking rear echelon medical attention, I'd bugged out so to speak, though it had an honorable face. The hurtfully wounded in the hospital appeared to disagree.

The Doctor let me read his notes: 'Ear drums perforated, tinnitus bilateral. Reprofile. Return to line unit.' It was succinct enough. I asked about 'reprofile' but was told to see Division Personnel about it.

Held over for transportation up to the MLR, I was billeted in a Divisional HQ tent. The opulence put me in mind of a visiting circus setting amidst the county fairgrounds. It was a big midway of clean fatigues and spit shined boots. I looked for a Ferris wheel, for race horses. I saw a marvel of logistics, a self sufficient mobile town that stayed in place as long as we infantrymen held the MLR. It was an amazing community: officers of all ranks, accountants, typists, physicians, cooks, quartermasters, truckers, all living in tents and huts with wooden floors, stoves, and generator powered electric lights. It was a behind the line spectacle I must have viewed upon arrival in Korea, but couldn't now recall, not even an iota of the colorful quarters. Sandbagged air raid shelters were evidence that roustabouts, probably quad-fifties, protected a field division's bureaucrats from the ravages of bedcheck Charley's occasional bomb.

 I felt the country bumpkin in a big city seeing ornate furnishings and accommodations forgotten at Kumhwa and on the Punchbowl. My nose detected the odor of sweet frying bacon. If only I could taste some bacon covered with eggs over easy. The whole place was tantalizingly irresistible. Yet there were drawbacks. Rear echelon types had longer time to pull in Korea to rotate, but it might well be worth it. I walked on gravel paths toward the Division's personnel tent.

 I saluted the lean soldier sitting behind a desk and reported, "Sergeant James F. Walsh, 35th Regiment, Dog Company." A smiling corporal neatly dressed, creases in his pressed fatigues, rose and extended his hand. So did I. Hands shaken he pointed me to a chair, and took his own. "I'm sorry, but I don't hear too well at the moment," I said. "You'll have to speak loudly."

The Corporal didn't speak but wrote: 'I was informed by the Hospital you were coming. I pulled and read your records. I'm Bill Purtell. You can't imagine how surprised I was to read you attended St Mary's Seminary at Mundelein, Illinois. So did my brother, Jim. Same time as you.'

I instantly saw the facial resemblance of Jim to Bill. Body types were different. Jim was a pudge of a man, bright as the sun, jolly as Santa. "We were classmates caught up in the Mickey Spillane Pocket Book scandal. The Seminary's Spiritual Director, 'Sparky', wanted all to quit the seminary who dared read detective stories instead of philosophical tomes. I refused to cooperate with the inquisition, but Jim and Mike Needham did. They quit. I transferred to St. Mary's Seminary in San Antonio, then quit in November. Afterwards, Jim, Mike, my brother Jack and I drank many a beer at the Cicero Hut in salute to Mickey Spillane. I was there at Jim's wedding to Betty. The good old days."

Purtell wrote, 'I missed the wedding. Just drafted. Not Jim. Enough that one Purtell is here.' Another note was written. 'About reprofile. I can get you off line and back to Battalion. Your two years in College should get you a clerkship.'

I read it. My head did a negative. "No thank you Bill. Return me to Dog. "Purtell's tent had comfort I'd deemed impossible for anyone other than had Shoemaker, my machine gun Section Sergeant. There were little houseboys everywhere doing the chores an infantryman takes for granted: cleaning weapons and equipment. Those little mice-like boys were making beds, folding clothes, doing all the things a well-to-do family hired a housemaid for. Even basic training in Camp Breckenridge's wooden barracks didn't have the down home comfort of division's HQ troops.

'Have a beer,' Purtell wrote. He lifted a towel from a tub filled with can's chilled by chunk ice. It was cold in Korea, and ice aplenty would be available in the polluted pools and paddies if a GI elected usage, but Purtell's was manufactured. I marveled at it. I was as surprised at the plentitude of beer. There had to be a couple of dozen cans. It was a horde to delight my thirsty throat, but I remembered my manners. I gave thanks to the benefactor, put a smile in the can's lid with the ever trusty P-38, and chug-a-lugged its contents.

Purtell offered another, glad that the friend of his brother was so thankful for such a slight luxury.

"I'll drink you dry if you keep being the nice guy," I said.

His gestures invited me to do just that, surprised at the reluctance.

I nodded a 'no', my face displaying reluctance. "It must have taken you two months to save up such a horde. I have to trade issued cigarettes or pay a buck a can. I wouldn't feel right."

Purtell drafted a reply. He handed it over. "No horde. We get all the beer we can drink." He showed me several deposits of cold beer; even a half dozen jugs of the hard stuff, much more than Shoemaker ever obtained, no one knew how. I took a long look at the big brow, small chinned Chicagoan whose heart was so kind he hadn't realized there was a negative in the plethora of distilled spirits at HQ. He simply hadn't been up to a line outfit where regiment's supply of beer was halved; battalions' quartered; line troops recipients of but a trickle down of seven cans a man per week! I dared not insult my host. I thanked him as he left to return to duty, while I set about diminishment of the brewer's art. After all, Corporal Purtell had nothing to do with the mal-distribution of the Army's scarce resources.

Of course, a combat troop in action shouldn't be drunk, but hadn't it been Civil War folklore, while leading an attack, General U. S. Grant hurled bottles of booze forward? Nothing was fair in life or the Army, but this distribution of beer was deliberate discrimination. I drank all I could!

Was I dreaming I heard a tenor somewhere singing 'Ode to Joy', an organ picking up the melody and accompaniment? My blurred eyes focused on the long greenish canvas spread above me. I saw a baby-faced boy in baggy GI fatigues smiling down on me, a cherub type that sat around the throne of God. The singing was so moving, I sensed I must be back in the seminary chapel. My soul glowed. I hadn't died! I hurt too much to have died. I'd just partied too long, waking with an elephant size head.

There were troops around a pock-face short stature soldier barely bigger than the houseboy he hugged. I heard the noise of the sideshow and discernible voices, a considerable auditory improvement since before my drinking binge. Beer obviously had medicinal qualities never before realized. Spotting Purtell, I asked, "what's going on with that stumpy troop and the kid?"

His note had but four words: 'Rotation. Thirty-four points'.

"Thirty-four," I shouted. "What happened to thirty-six? Warren's's got more than thirty-four and he's still on the hill! What going on?" The whole of the tent's rear echelon were startled at my thundering. No wonder. They saw a twisted visage, the shape of terror, a demon up on woozy feet. I fixed bayonet on my carbine. "I'm going to jab that little pock-faced punk. He's favored himself and messed with Warren. No little pimple puss of a rear echelon crud is going home when men in Korea before him are left up on the MLR."

    I staggered forward to thrust steel when typists, accountants, auditors, personnel clerks, even supply sergeants came from all sides to grapple with me, a raving lunatic turned maniac. I was forced to the tent's wooden floor where half a dozen fought to restrain me. A medic with a syringe full of horse tranquilizer, I later suspected, drove a knife-like needle deeply within my left arm.

    When the effects of the sleep producing drug wore off, I was back at Dog Company, not in a Military Police Guard House. I supposed because none at Division rear wanted the motivation behind my bayonet work, insufficient as it was, made known to a Court Martial.

NIGHT GUARD IN DOG TWO BUNKER

North of the 38th parallel Korea is a mountainous area with long ridge lines and slopes that run down from the peak of hills like fingers from a hand.

My outfit, the 35th Regimental Combat team of the 25th Infantry Division was dug in on a forward slope of the Punch Bowl in North Korea facing the Chinese. Our section of heavy machine guns formed a part of the Main Line of Resistance. As squad leader, I had placed our guns down a finger to get maximum fire power where our commander anticipated the enemy would most likely hit.

In the Autumn of 1951 we had launched attacks against the North Koreans and the Chinese inflicting numerous casualties while suffering only a few ourselves. Then, in the late fall we were ordered to dig in. We were elated to think that this was it - the end of the war and combat - that we would need only to man the trenches. That was not to be.

Every enlisted man in the Army knows an officer is specifically assigned the duty of finding things that do not have to be done and thus can be done over and over again by the GI. Obviously this Officer informed our commander that GIs should not merely man trenches, but they should run large-scale combat patrols to prove to the enemy they have not lost their will to fight. The combat patrols were full-scale operations. We would take the high point and continue to shoot into the enemy, who by then were bugging out, going down several different fingers. Then our commanders had us abandon the hill. Within a few days the enemy would invariably reoccupy it. Several weeks later, we would roar out again, retake the hill, hold it as long as the commander wanted and then pull out.

The Chinese were not inactive themselves. Not to be outdone, their infiltrators would silently penetrate our lines and kidnap any UN soldier they could get. Rumors of such Chinese successes were rampant.

Both side must have been equally disgusted with the number of rats around the bunkers. These rodents seemed to thrive on the war and increased and multiplied when we entered trench warfare. We weren't paid to shoot them, but from time to time we squeezed off a round. It was a losing battle.

Once, as I thought the rats had more replacements than the Chinese, I turned around to the sound of angry voices. Section leader, First Sergeant Warren was coming down the trench from the line with his carbine drawn and a GI in front of him. The soldier was letting out a series of vile phrases directed at the United States Army and Warren. My squad came out of the bunkers and gathered at Dog Two gun hole.

"Hey, Red, this guy is your new replacement. Keep the crud. If he so much as leaves the bunker, shoot him for bugging out," Warren exploded.

At that, the new guy let out another alliteration of vulgarity about Warren's lineage. Warren clicked off the safety of his weapon. Half the squad jumped the sergeant and hassled him up the trench to the line. The rest of the squad hustled the new guy into the Dog Two sleeping bunker.

George told us his name. He had just come from stateside, where as a civilian he had been a truck driver. He claimed he should be in the motor pool. That line duty was a dirty deal. He was visibly shaking.

I introduced myself to George, then to all the guys in the squad, telling him we manned three machine gun bunkers on the finger. Clouse, Gzregorek and I were to the left in Dog One bunker. Brooks, Alexander and Truscott were in Dog Three bunker to the right. I told Rosenbloom that George would be assigned to him and Im Ta Song in the Dog Two bunker in the center.

Rosenbloom couldn't leave well enough alone. "Hey, George. You know what? Damn Chinese infiltrated just over there. Easy Company. Four days ago, they kidnaped a GI," Rosenbloom said as he pointed his thumb over his shoulder at some undetermined place.

There was a long silence in the bunker. George looked at me, then at Rosey and then at Im Ta Song. It was as if he had seen Im for the first time. "Who's that?" George expressed a few cogent opinions about people of South Korean descent. He became highly agitated again, shaking nervously and his Adam's apple bouncing like a fishing bob.

"Yep. Just four days ago Chinese got a guy right up there." Rosenbloom's point appeared to be to Dog Three bunker.

There was another long silence. George's eyes were white, watery and wide.

It made little difference to Rosenbloom that George was so distraught when he put him on first night guard. It is to the advantage of sleeping buddies that the night guard be highly alert. This night the wind was whooshing and whistling over the line and down drafts played about the bunkers, popping ponchos covering their entrances. The rear echelon search lights came across the line to light up the clouds over no man's land. The light reflected downward, illuminating both sides of the line and increasing shadows and anxiety. As the clouds moved, the light walked across the valley and changed known forms into unknown.

    We had hung C-ration cans on the barbed wire to rattle if disturbed by the enemy. A particularly good wind would rattle a can and even an experienced GI's imagination could be so terrorized that he would whistle an alert over the communication telephone. That was always followed by a parachute flare, then a coarse request to settle down and let the command bunker sleep.

    Brooks came on guard in Dog Three bunker and I in Dog One during the forth shift, while Im Ta Song was forcing George back again on guard with a torrent of impolite Korean phrases. Rosey awoke and cursed George mightily, venting all his feelings about being awaken seven times on George's first shift.

    The rats were out in force this night. They slipped around the side of my bunker and ran along the top of the commo trench up towards Dog Two. George had not been informed of the rats. Rosenbloom's indoctrination covered the gun holes, communication system and other soldierly duties befalling a line troop, but he forgot to mention our rats. This particular night they seemed to sense an intense element of fear from Dog Two and they apparently called a convention at the site. Coming through the roof at the gun bunker, they knocked dirt onto George's helmet. He jumped and his helmet fell. The startled rats jumped in response. George gasped loudly as he sucked in air. He sounded as if he had been choked.

When Brooks heard the gasp, he came out of his gun hole to look down the trench towards Dog Two. "Whatsamatter down there? Whatsgoing on? George?"

The rats fled the roof, jumping to the sides of the gun bunker, and scurried out of the shooting port past George. Their sudden movement, and man's instinctive dislike for rats, and the soldier's for surprise, combined to cause George to tear the air with a loud guttural sob.

Brooks figured the Chinese had the new guy and hurled an illuminating grenade down the communication trench. It burst right by Dog Two bunker. George saw the explosion and let out a piercing cry.

I was looking out the gun port down the finger towards the Chinese lines when I caught the flash of the illuminating grenade. I grabbed my carbine.

When Brooks heard the cry, he had visions of the Chinese carrying George down the finger to their lines. He couldn't see anyone so he rolled a fragmentation grenade down the trench. It exploded and zinged fragments through the air.

George, thinking he was fleeing the infiltrating Chinese, ran from the bunker and up the commo trench away from the line. Brooks saw the fleeting figure and cut loose with his M2 carbine. The whole line came to life and some fire erupted from different gun holes.

I was just starting to get up from the trench floor after the fragmentation grenade, when the M2 started popping my way. I hit the ground again.

Brooks yelled down to Dog Two. "Whatsamatter down there? George?"

"What you doing, Brooks?" I yelled.

Rosenbloom had been blown nearly out of his bunk at the grenade explosion and was coming out of the sleeping bunker with Im Ta Song when the carbine cut loose. They fell back into the hole. Then Rosenbloom heard Brooks call and my calling out to Brooks.

Rosenbloom yelled out to us: "For the love of Mike, we're on your side. Stop shooting."

Both Brooks and I worked our way to Dog Two. Rosey came out cautiously. We didn't see George. "They got George," Brooks said.

"What the hell are you talking about?" I asked. Brooks told of the gasp and the sob, the fleeting figure and why he threw the grenades and fired his weapon. I put the squad on 100 % alert and whistled the phone to get the command post to tell them Brook's story. The whole company was put on 100 % alert and a squad sent down the finger to look for George and any Chinese patrol. They returned an hour later with no signs of any activity. We pulled the rest of night guard on alert.

About dawn,, heading to the straddle crapper, I saw George coming out of the section's reverse slope bunker wrapped in a blanket like a hot dog in a bun.

Rosenbloom now has another replacement. He was told about the rats.

George liked it back at the Regimental Motor Pool.

HOMECOMING

When time for rotation came up, 36 points, (nine months with a MLR combat outfit), I still hadn't overcome my feelings of stupidity for crawling down and up slope with two Chinamen through barbed and concertina wire around a booby trapped mine field. I did when I turned down the Top Kick's offer to forsake rotation for three more months with Dog Company and, in return, the Section Sergeant of the 3rd section and the double rockers of a Sergeant First Class; six weeks later the triple rockers of a Master Sergeant. No deal! I rotated to the good old USA in May 1952, an alive, very bright, single rocker U. S. Army Staff Sergeant.

It took two weeks for the troop ship to cross the Pacific Ocean. When it docked at San Francisco's Presidio, it nearly keeled over, every GI who could, crowding the rails dockside. We looked for the welcoming committee, a band, the Red Cross with coffee and donuts.

There was no crowd, no band, no Red Cross, no coffee or donuts, nothing to welcome America's fighting men home from Korea in late May 1952. There was a collective grunt for ingratitude. The ship's unloading ramp hit the landing, and GIs, thrilled to be back on American soil while irritated they'd been forgotten, filed cheerfully toward the reception building. From out of nowhere, three civilians, a beautiful young woman dressed prettier than a fashion model, an older pretty woman as sharply dressed holding the hand of an older handsome man in a black serge suit and red tie rushed onto the landing. A GI broke ranks, dropped his equipment and ran from the ramp into the arms of his sweetheart, his parents. They hugged and kissed, kissed and hugged, hugged and kissed. There wasn't a dry GI eye aboard ship or on the landing.

    I had in mind a reception of my own. After I'd arrived at Fort Sheridan, Illinois and got my orders for leave, I was going to catch a Chicago bus, get off in front of St. Juliana School, pull my kid brother out of grade school and march two blocks of Oketo Street to home and a surprise on Mom and Dad. It was I who was surprised. At the gates of Fort Sheridan, there were Mom, Dad, sister Kay and brothers Jack, Ed and Denny.

    There wasn't a dry GI eye.

SEPARATION

The time for my active duty enlistment had run in November 1952. I was now in the inactive reserve, back home in Chicago and looking around for a college to attend. Was it to be Northwestern or Notre Dame?

Dad had an answer. "I've the papers, Jim, commissioning you a Lieutenant in the Irish Republican Army. Your ticket to Ireland is in the mail. You'll train the lads in the north in combat techniques."

I'd sipped two many beers. They must have effected my hearing even more than usual. "What?"

"We've got weapons in the hands of Catholic lads willing to use them to drive the Protestants out of Ulster. You'll teach tactics."

"Teach tactics to Catholics! Drive Protestants out! Dad, who do you think was beside me for nine months of combat in Korea? Protestants! My Section Sergeant, squad leader, assistant gunner, 1st ammo bearer and on and on and on and on. Protestants! I'm not now about to teach Catholics to kill Protestants, much less in Ireland. I'm an American!"

Dad's face turned tense, lips curled, drawn around cutting teeth.

I'd committed an act of ancestral treason, not forgotten by Dad even when I enrolled at the home of the Fighting Irish.

ACKNOWLEDGEMENTS

The Author would like to gratefully acknowledge an outstanding young woman, his granddaughter Rita Stradling, whose skills not limited to design, formatting and computer expertise are of enormous assistance in bringing this memoir out of the family cupboard to Amazon.com.

Thank you Rita.

Along with being my granddaughter, Rita Stradling is the author of The Deception Dance series which is also available on Amazon.com.

www.ingramcontent.com/pod-product-compliance
Lightning Source LLC
Chambersburg PA
CBHW070621300426
44113CB00010B/1610